THE 16 STRIVINGS FOR GOD

THE

16

STRIVINGS
FOR GOD

THE NEW PSYCHOLOGY OF RELIGIOUS EXPERIENCES

STEVEN REISS

MERCER UNIVERSITY PRESS | MACON, GEORGIA

MUP/ H911

© 2015 Steven Reiss

Published by Mercer University Press
1501 Mercer University Drive
Macon, Georgia 31207
All rights reserved

9 8 7 6 5 4 3 2 1

Books published by Mercer University Press are printed on
acid-free paper that meets the requirements
of the American National Standard for Information Sciences—
Permanence of Paper for Printed Library Materials.

Text design by Burt&Burt

ISBN 978-0-88146-557-0

Cataloging-in-Publication Data is available from the Library of Congress

*"It takes all of us
to spell out the meaning
of spirituality."*

William James
VARIETIES OF RELIGIOUS EXPERIENCE

DEDICATION

On an ordinary workday in October 1995, I went to an outpatient clinic because I was feeling tired and couldn't regain normal energy.

The clinic was located about 100 yards from my office at The Ohio State University Medical Center. The physician who saw me that day noticed some jaundice and referred me for a procedure called ERCP, which basically produces images of liver ducts. When I awoke after the procedure, my physician told me I had a fatal autoimmune disease and would need a liver transplant within months.

The news was shocking. I had never been seriously ill before and I had no idea what a liver transplant was. At first blush I didn't understand how anyone could survive such an operation; I feared I would die in the operating room. "Everyone wakes up after a liver transplant," my surgeon assured me, "and at least gets to go home."

With additional medical evaluations, the news went from very bad to much worse. The doctors had images of what appeared to be tumors, one in each of the two main liver ducts feeding the common pathway. These are typically cancer tumors. Biliary cancer is a death sentence with survival rates of a half year or so. My physicians weren't certain that the images on their films were in fact tumors, but the odds were high.

In 1995 public policy prohibited transplanting most patients with cancer because the immunosuppressant drugs needed after organ transplantation diminish patients' resistance to the spread of cancer. I faced the prospect of undergoing a liver transplant operation—with all the pain, stress, and bother associated with that operation—only to wake up after the operation and be told that the transplant was called off because once the surgeons got a look inside, they verified I had cancer and called off the operation.

The prospect of having a transplant operation called off after I was opened up was too much for me to cope with. I had to know if I had cancer. At University Hospital in Cleveland, a unit of Case Western Reserve University, Dr. Michael Sivak was experimenting with flexible probes and thought he could get a camera right to where the films indicated tumors were located. He could then determine if they were cancerous.

As they wheeled me into a large procedure room in October 1995, I was frightened to death. I knew the odds were very high that within an hour my life expectancy would be assessed at about six months. I was 55 years old. The large procedure room had about 40 doctors in it. More were watching on cameras at locations throughout the country. About 30 minutes after the procedure started, a roar of cheers and applause woke me up. The probes had arrived at where the films indicated tumors were but there were no tumors. There was no tumor in the right duct, and there was no tumor in the left duct. It was just a bunch of crushed stones, which Dr. Sivak proceeded to remove. Within three hours I was on my way home, hoping I mightn't even need a transplant, but believing that if I did, I would get one because I was cancer-free. Dr. Sivak's experimental procedure gave me seven mostly healthy years from 1995 to 2002.

On August 1, 2002, a young man I never met named Paul passed away in a hospital somewhere in Ohio. In death Paul did something very important, namely, he donated life to dying patients who had rushed to hospitals throughout Ohio to await his gifts. In the early morning hours of August 2, Elmahdi Elkhammas, M.D., led a team of transplant surgeons who removed my diseased liver and replaced it with Paul's still healthy liver. Ten days later I returned home with Paul's liver working to heal the surgical wounds and restore my body to sound health. I don't know how many lives Paul saved in the early hours of August 2; I only know I was one of them.

This book is dedicated to those who give life to people they do not even know—that is, the book is dedicated to everyone who is a registered organ donor—and to organ transplant physicians and nurses everywhere, but most especially this book is for Paul and the surgeons and nurses who gave me life twelve and a half years ago.

THE

16

STRIVINGS
FOR GOD

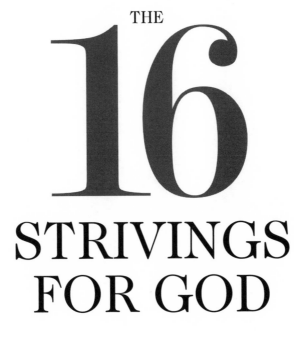

1

THE RAISON D'ETRE
FOR RELIGION

Augustine of Hippo (1964/397) thought that religion is about worshipping the God of the Bible, who is the Creator of everything including mankind (Russell, 1972). He believed that religion began because God revealed himself in Holy Scriptures. Although these ideas may seem obvious to some, many scholars have suggested otherwise, or at least thought there is much more to be said on the topic. Worldwide many religious people do not believe in a deity resembling the Judeo-Christian God. Buddhists, for example, do not worship a Creator. Since not all of the world's major religions worship God, some scholars have thought that the essence of religion must be about something else.

What is the essence of religion if not worshipping God? Here we will learn that scholars have suggested a number of different answers to this question. Each answer, known in scholarship as a theory of religion, suggests why religion emerged and became influential. Most cite one or two aspects of human nature as having given rise to religion. Some scholars suggested, for example, that religion arose to address the need to understand who we are, whereas others argued that religion is about morality, and still others suggested that religion is an effort to cope with the fear of death. In this chapter we will review briefly the various theories of religion. Our aim is to provide the context for the new theory of religion introduced in this book, called "the 16 strivings for God".

Despite centuries of scholarly debate aimed at identifying the raison d'etre for religion, my own view is that religion has no single essence but is multifaceted. Many of the previous theories of religion are invalid because they are narrowly focused on just one or two needs of human nature when in reality religion addresses a wide range of human needs. Some people may embrace God as Creator, but religion is about much more than explaining who we are and how we got here. Some might practice religion to reduce their fear of death, but religion is about much more than managing anxiety and fear. The multifaceted nature of religion may seem apparent, but it isn't or scholars would not have spent centuries searching for its essence.

NEED FOR UNDERSTANDING

Edward Burnett Tylor (1881), a nineteenth century anthropologist, suggested that religion emerged as an effort to understand the universe. At the dawn of civilization, Tylor believed, people were bewildered by life and tried to make sense of it. They wondered about the possibility of afterlife, what causes illness, why rivers flow, and so on. They embraced a childish form of thinking called animism, according to which supernatural spirits move plants, animals, rivers, mountains, and other objects. Why was the village struck by outbreaks of illness? According to animism, it is because the members of the tribe were possessed by demons. Why did the volcano explode? Because the mountain god was angry.

Tylor viewed animism as the forerunner of religion because it sustained belief in supernatural spirits. To support his thesis, he showed that animism is found in many primitive societies dating back to the dawn of history.

From a psychological standpoint, Tylor's theory of animism implies that the intellectual need for understanding is the true origin of religion. In Chapter 2 we will learn that this need is just one of 16 psychological needs driving the human psyche. It is distinct from, and largely unrelated to, other psychological needs (Reiss, 2013a). Tylor's ideas may help us understand how religion expresses our need for understanding, but religion encompasses much more than creation myths.

The human need for understanding is at most only one of a number of factors that gave rise to religion. If religion had in fact emerged as an expression of this need, as Tylor's theory implies, it would have appealed primarily to the relatively small proportion of humans who are intellectuals. Sure, non-intellectuals wonder where they come from or how the universe was created or why volcanoes erupt, but many do not wonder about these matters for any length of time. Since we are not an intellectual species, a religion that is essentially intellectual in origin or nature is unlikely ever to gain a mass following.

Religion encompasses much more than just the intellectual aspects of life. It also addresses, for example, ritual, fear, and morality. It is much too popular and diverse to be explained as an expression of the intellectual need for understanding.

NEED FOR CONTROL

James George Fraser (2009/1890), who also was an anthropologist, suggested that religion arose in part from a need to control natural events essential to survival. Primitive people needed a supply of animals to kill for meat, fertile soil and rain to grow their crops, and protection from natural disasters. Yet they often had little control over natural disasters, illnesses, weather, and other crucial events that might prevent them from finding food, shelter, and safety.

In his book *The Golden Bough: A Study in Comparative Religion,* Fraser discussed magic and religion. He noted that "witch doctors" claimed special access or knowledge of the spirits and alleged they knew how to consult them for favors such as a successful hunt, good crops, health, and so on. The witch doctors practiced magic to influence the spirits who they claimed animate and control the world. Magic flourished in primitive societies. Some scholars say that religion emerged from the teachings of medicine men regarding magic.

Whereas Tylor implied that the human desire for understanding gave rise to religion, Fraser's discussion of magic gave emphasis to the desire for control. The results of our research on psychological needs—presented in the next chapter of this book— show that the needs for understanding and control are distinct and largely unrelated aspects of human nature.

Individuals motivated to embrace religion for understanding, and those motivated to embrace religion for control, are driven by different psychological needs and values. The desire for understanding motivates curiosity, while the desire for control motivates assertiveness. If they were the same need, curious people would tend to be assertive and vice versa. They are not. Many curious people are not controlling, or dominant personality types. Many assertive people are not at all curious. This suggests that understanding and control are two largely unrelated psychological needs.

Religion is about much more than a need to control our environments. If religion were about control, assertive people, who report a strong need for control, would be more religious than are laid-back people, who report a weak need for control. They are not. How religious a person is has little to do with the extent to which the person values or is seeking to control the environment or important life events.

NEED FOR HONOR

Did religion emerge because it encourages moral behavior, which is essential for social life? Philosopher Hastings Rashdall (1964/1907) suggested that morality is the essence of religion. He thought that religion is needed to justify right from wrong. The philosopher Immanuel Kant (1998/ 1781) argued that a belief in God is needed to make denial of self-interest a rational, moral choice.

In terms of the 16 psychological needs discussed in this book, morality falls under the need for honor. If morality were the essence of religion, honorable people should be more religious than are expedient people. According to the results of some research studies (Reiss, 2000b), this implication may be true. The results of our studies suggest that the need for honor motivates the flock to embrace religion, and the need for idealism motivates the clergy. Much more research is needed, however, to study these issues before we can draw firm conclusions.

NEED FOR SAFETY

Psychiatrist Sigmund Freud argued that religion is about coping with anxiety and fear, especially the fear of death. Many influential scholars, such as the twentieth century philosopher Bertrand Russell, also thought that the fear of death gave rise to religion. Social psychologists have reported experiments in which reminders of death temporarily increase people's faith in supernatural agents (Vail *et al.*, 2010).

The fact that primitive societies invented a god for virtually every important catastrophe that might befall them is strong evidence that one of the psychological functions of religion is the management of fear. Primitive people made sacrifices to their gods in exchange for protection from whatever it was they feared. Farmers, for example, worshipped agricultural gods who had powers to bless them with bountiful crops or curse them with famine. Warriors imagined gods of battle who could bless them with victory or curse them with defeat. The priesthood taught the faithful to worship and make sacrifices to the gods in exchange for being blessed and protected. This had the psychological benefit of reducing fear and anxiety for those who believed.

Sigmund Freud (1950/1913; 1989/1927) thought that religion is about the management of anxiety and fear. Actually, he thought that virtually everything people think or do is motivated by efforts to manage anxiety and fear. To support his thesis, Freud called attention to presentations of God as a protective father figure. In his book *Future of an Illusion,* Freud speculated that religion arises in part from the infant's experience of helplessness and yearning for a protector. When adults face danger or deprivation, they imagine a god who looks out for them the way their parents did when they were young. They project onto this god the qualities of the father: loving, stern, and protective. Freud suggested that religious beliefs are motivated in part by the wish to have a father figure in heaven who takes care of us, protects us from harm, and punishes us to keep us in line.

The view that religion is primarily about managing fear and anxiety has at least three major problems with it. One, this theory implies that anxious people are attracted to religion more than are non-anxious people, and they aren't. Although artificially arousing the fear of death in laboratories motivates people to embrace religious beliefs, in everyday life the people who worry the most about dying aren't necessarily the ones who are most religious.

Two, some religious beliefs and practices increase fear of death. If the people who invented religion were seeking to build a congregation by helping the flock cope with the fear of death, surely they would have left out of their theology the fires of hell. The prospect of burning in hell for eternity increases the fear of death. Similarly, the concepts of the devil and judgment day increase anxiety and fear.

Three, Freud's view that religious rituals are motivated by anxiety reduction is dubious and invalidly exaggerates the role of anxiety and fear in religious beliefs and practices. In 1907 Freud famously suggested that religious rituals are compulsions, or symptoms of Obsessive-Compulsive Disorder (OCD). He called religion a universal obsessional neurosis. He claimed that the same unconscious mental processes cause both compulsions and rituals. "The parallelism," wrote Catherine Bell (2000), "led to the conclusion that one might describe neurosis as an individual religiosity and religion as a universal neurosis" (p. 13).

I disagreed with Freud's analysis in my 2008 book entitled *The Normal Personality: A New Way of Thinking about People*. Although OCD symptoms, such as compulsive cleanliness, are motivated by anxiety reduction, I think religious rituals typically are motivated by the psychological need for order. In my view, people embrace rituals because they structure their lives and increase predictability and stability. Religious rituals address the psychological need for order and, thus, are not about the need to manage anxiety.

NEED FOR ORDER

William Robertson Smith (1894) thought that rituals were the raison d'etre for religion. Karen Armstrong (2009) suggested that rituals unlock the spiritual meaning of a wide spectrum of ancient and modern cultural activities. In order to discover religion's truth, wrote Armstrong, we need to translate religious doctrines into ritual. Religious rituals include prayer and the ceremonial rites practiced during Church services (Bell, 2000).

Religion is about much more than rituals and the human need for order. Although practicing a religion structures one's life, religion also addresses other human needs such as understanding, control, and anxiety management.

MYSTICISM

According to William James (2004/1902), the essence of religion is personal experience of the Absolute, commonly known as mysticism. He held that "personal religious experience has its root and center in mystical states of consciousness" (p. 329). What is mysticism? It is an experience in which one senses the presence of an awesome, transcendental reality, as if one's soul or consciousness had been absorbed into God. As James Pratt (1921) explained, "It is a sense or feeling of this presence, not the belief in it, and it is not the result of sight or hearing or touch, nor is it a conclusion one reaches by thought; it is, instead, an immediate intuitive experience" (p. 337).

James is just one of many scholars who regarded mysticism as a core religious experience. In her book *The Case for God*, Karen Armstrong (2009) observed that mysticism is found in all major religions and is especially prominent in eastern religious traditions. According to the theory introduced in this book, mysticism is motivated partially by uncommonly high valuations of harmony and interdependence.

Carl Jung (1923) observed that in western religions such as Christianity, God is experienced as an "object," or a reality separate from the soul. In eastern religions such as Buddhism, God is experienced from the soul, as a subject rather than an object. Jung regarded the eastern approach to be more meaningful.

TRANSCENDENCE

Some scholars have suggested that religion is an effort to unify the divided self. Whereas philosophers divided human nature into mind and body, psychologists divided the mind into conscious and unconscious parts.

Reinhold Niebuhr (1949), a protestant theologian, suggested that religion is rooted in man's dual nature. Although our bodies are part of the physical world, Niebuhr thought that certain aspects of our psyche—notably free choice, morality, the use of symbols, self-consciousness, memory, and love—give us glimpses of something greater than the physical world. The hints of a greater reality motivate us to search for the God who transcends the world.

NEED FOR STATUS

Emil Durkheim (1965/1915), the father of sociology, held that religions distinguish between the sacred and the profane. Sacred things are superior, powerful, and entitled to great respect. Profane things are ordinary, uneventful, and routine. "Religion," wrote Durkheim, "is a unified system of beliefs and practices relative to sacred things...." (quoted Pals, 2006, p. 960).

Although Durkheim believed that religion cannot be reduced to psychological needs, I suggest that from a psychological standpoint, the distinction between sacred and profane is an expression of a universal need for status. As a psychologist, I would interpret Durkheim as suggesting that religion addresses the need for status even though Durkheim himself rejected such psychological reductionism.

NEED FOR SOCIAL CONTACT

Durkheim also held that religion is a collective, communal experience. He thought that religious rituals and ceremonies provide opportunities for the community to assemble and share extraordinary and moving experiences. This suggests that one of the psychological functions of religion is to help satisfy the need for social contact.

In summary, various scholars asserted that religion became popular because it explained the universe; promised to enhance control of our environments; encouraged morality; made people feel safe in a world fraught with danger; offered rituals that enhanced the sense of order and reduced the sense of chaos; embraced mystical experiences of the Absolute; addressed the divided self by encouraging us to embrace transcendental reality; distinguished between the sacred and the profane; and strengthened the sense of belonging to tribal communities. Although previous scholars debated which one of these needs was most important for the origin of religion, no one need is widely accepted to be the single essence of religion. In my view there is no single, overarching need driving people to religion. In this book I will make the case that religion is essentially multifaceted and that it is too rich an experience to be reduced to just one aspect of life. Religion addresses a wide range of human needs, or meaningful experiences, not just one need or psychological source of meaning.

2

THE 16 BASIC DESIRES OF HUMAN NATURE

William McDougall (2003/1908) observed that we all want the same things from life and are moved by the same goals. He wrote,

> Every man is so constituted to seek, to strive for, and to desire certain goals which are common to the species, and the attainment of which goals satisfies and allays the urge or craving or desire that moves us. These goals... are not only common to all men, but also... [to] their nearer relatives in the animal world; such goals as food; shelter from danger, the company of our fellows; intimacy with the opposite sex, triumph over our opponents, and leadership among our companions (pp. 406–407).

Four generations of Harvard University psychologists studied universal motives, but with different semantics. Both William James (1918/1890) and William McDougall (2003/1908) called them "human instincts" to suggest they evolved from primates. Henry Murray (1938) and David McClelland (1961) called them "psychological needs" to imply involvement of the unconscious mind. I prefer the term "basic desire" to give emphasis to the conscious, subjective experience of a universal motive. Nevertheless, in this book I will use the terms "universal motive," "universal goal," "human instinct," "basic desire," and "psychological need" interchangeably.

What are the basic desires common to everyone and deeply rooted in human nature? Can we generate a list of universal motives? Actually psychologists used a variety of methods to list out what we all want, or as it is sometimes worded, what makes us tick. McDougall (2003/1908), for example, relied on anthropological accounts of primitive societies. He suggested the following nine basic desires:

- Flight from danger
- Repulsion from pain
- Curiosity or wonder about new places or things
- Pugnacity when angered or threatened
- Parenting (protecting and cherishing the young)
- Self-abasement (or subjection) when feeling negatively about oneself
- Self-display when in the presence of spectators
- Gregariousness (herd instinct) when lonely
- Sex (reproduction) when aroused

On the other hand, Murray (1938) used story-telling techniques to assess the unconscious desires of Harvard undergraduates. He identified 20 needs but admitted that his list "is not very different from lists constructed by McDougall, Garnett, and a number of other writers" (p. 84) who did not study the unconscious mind. Murray's 20 needs are as follows:

- Abasement, the need to surrender and accept punishment
- Achievement, the need to overcome obstacles and succeed
- Affiliation, the need for friendships
- Aggression, the need to injure others

- Autonomy, the need to resist others and stand strong
- Counteraction, the need to defend honor
- Defendance, the need to justify actions
- Deference, the need to follow a superior
- Dominance, the need to control and lead others
- Exhibition, the need for attention
- Harmavoidance, the need to avoid pain
- Infavoidance, the need to avoid failure/shame or conceal weakness
- Nurturance, the need to protect the helpless
- Order, the need to arrange, organize, and be precise
- Play, the need to relieve tension, have fun, or relax
- Rejection, the need to exclude another
- Sentience, the need for sensuality
- Sex, the need for erotic relationships
- Succorance, the need for support
- Understanding, the need to analyze and know

Abraham Maslow (1943, 1954), who taught at Brandeis University only a few miles from Harvard, studied psychological needs of well-adjusted, or self-actualized, people. He published the influential idea of a "hierarchy" or "pyramid" of psychological needs.

By the 1960s psychologists had spent nearly seventy years studying psychological needs but had very little to show for it. They had produced many lists of needs, none scientifically valid. They had found few practical applications for the numerous lists of psychological needs. Murray's list of needs was used primarily in psychiatric diagnosis, but it was used much less often after 1980 when psychiatric diagnosis was overhauled. After 70 years of disappointing progress, clinical psychologists moved away from studying universal motives or needs and instead embraced behaviorism in the 1960s, cognitions in the 1970s, and neuropsychology in the 2000s.

OUR RESEARCH

My colleagues and I appear to be the first scholars to list out the universal motives deeply rooted in human nature by asking large numbers of people in scientifically valid surveys using a reliable and valid questionnaire. In the language of psychological research, we "empirically derived" a list of universal motives rather than just making one up and using our debating skills to argue for its validity. We did not follow in the footsteps of the instinct theorists and book trips to New Guinea or Africa. We did not follow in the footsteps of psychodynamic personality theorists and ask college students to make up stories or tell us what they see when looking at inkblots. We did not follow in the footsteps of Abraham Maslow and study in depth successful people. Instead, we constructed questionnaires that anonymously asked people about their motives, pursuits, and core values.

Many psychologists do not ask people questions like, "What motivates you?" "What are your values" "What are you trying to accomplish?" Psychologists pay little attention to conscious motives, core values, and goals. Instead, they ask people questions such as, "What happened when you were five? How did you feel about your father when you were a little child? Did you feel your mother loved you when you were four? What do you see in this inkblot?"

Although psychoanalysts and behaviorists are two groups of psychologists who famously disagree on what makes us tick, both groups believe we cannot understand behavior based on what people tell us about their motives and values. Both typically do not ask people about motives, purposes, and intentions. Freud (1963/1916) taught that people do not know what is really motivating them. He claimed that our important motives are unconscious thoughts and feelings we carry forward from childhood and now resist acknowledging.

B F. Skinner (1938), one of the fathers of behaviorism, held that human intentions and purposes are "explanatory fictions" that cannot be studied scientifically. He ignored human purposes and encouraged others to do the same. Behaviorists believe that the real causes of our actions are in the environment.

Further, many psychologists do not study human purposes because they expect people to answer the questions, "What are your motives? What are you trying to accomplish" with self-serving, self-deceiving untruths. They expect, for example, dishonest people to exaggerate how hard they try to be honest, and they expect lazy people to tell interviewers they work hard. Psychologists have been so negative on the validity of conscious motives that, in the 1990s when my colleagues and I surveyed thousands of people about their motives, we were criticized for listing out universal motivators (human needs) based on what people say are their values and purposes.

Even social psychologists have challenged the validity of self-reported motives (Deci, Koestner, & Ryan, 1999). They have argued that the best way to learn what motivates people is to observe what they do, not what they say. If you want to know if a college man likes puzzles, for example, don't ask him, but watch to see if he plays with puzzles in leisurely circumstances when no extrinsic gains are anticipated. If you want to know if a girl likes to draw, don't ask her but watch to see if the child draws on her own when no extrinsic gains are anticipated. Valid? Not really. In my treatise *Myths of Intrinsic Motivation*, (Reiss, 2013b), I show that the social psychology method of inferring motives from behavior has multiple flaws and errors in logic. A college man who intrinsically likes puzzles, for example, might not play with them if he has opportunities to participate in activities he likes even more. A girl who hates drawing will spend all day doing so if the alternatives are disliked even more. Social psychologists got it backwards: The best and simplest way to learn how much people are intrinsically motivated by puzzles or drawing is to ask them, not to watch what they do.

As these comments suggest, researchers have exaggerated the limitations of questionnaires, or what they call self-report data. If you listen to enough research psychologists rattling off the short-comings of asking people about themselves, you might come to the conclusion it is a waste of time to ask anybody anything. Yet in everyday life, asking leads to very valuable information. And so it can be in rigorous psychological research as well. Although we need to be concerned about faking and distortion in questionnaire data, researchers can take well-established steps to reduce the risks.

My colleagues and I have executed a series of large-scale surveys of what people say motivates them. We have learned that asking people about their motives is usually a valid method for learning who they are and why they do what they do. How people answer our questionnaire corresponds to how they behave in everyday life. It predicts what they will try to do at home, work, school, sports, and so on.

So in the decade of the 1990s, when I had been diagnosed with a fatal autoimmune disease, I wondered what makes people tick. I kept coming back to McDougall's idea of universal motives. I agreed fully that certain desires are common to everyone and deeply rooted in human nature. To list out these goals, I decided I would ask people about their motives and values. I invited then graduate student Susan Havercamp to work with me on this ambitious project. With my health situation, I figured I had better get going on the research while I was still healthy enough to do it.

In a series of scientific studies, Susan Havercamp and I presented diverse groups of people with hundreds of possible goals and asked them to rate the degree to which they embraced each one. In total about 7,700 people from diverse stations in life participated in our initial research surveys. Since the participants completed the questionnaire anonymously, they knew the information they gave could not be linked to them individually and could not be used against them. They had little reason to withhold truthful responses.

We discovered the 16 basic desires—the first scientifically derived list of psychological needs (Reiss & Havercamp, 1998, 2005). Readers who want to know the details of our research methods might look at my book, *The Reiss Motivation Profile* (Reiss, 2013a), or for easy reading, *Who Am I: The 16 Basic Desires That Motivate Our Actions and Define Our Personalities* (Reiss,

2000a). I will limit myself here to summarizing what readers need to know to understand the possible implications of the 16 basic desires for religion.

The 16 basic desires were discovered based on a mathematical technique, called factor analysis, of how the participants in our research surveys rated hundreds of diverse motives and goals. At the risk of oversimplification, what the research showed is that nearly all motives can be considered as combinations of one or more of 16 basic desires. If we know how someone rates the degree to which he or she embraces each of 16 basic desires, we can estimate the extent to which the individual pursues hundreds of possible goals.

Working independently of Susan and myself, Professor Ken Olson and his team at Fort Hays State University in Kansas validated the 16 basic desires in a series of scientific studies. They demonstrated correlations between the 16 basic desires and the Big 5 personality test and with other independently validated psychological tools (Olson & Chapin, 2007; Olson & Weber, 2004). As of this writing our research has produced the largest database of human motives ever collected. More than 100,000 people have completed our questionnaire, now called the Reiss Motivation Profile®.

THE 16 BASIC DESIRES ARE AS FOLLOWS:

- **Acceptance**, the desire for positive self-regard
- **Curiosity**, the desire for understanding
- **Eating**, the desire for food
- **Family**, the desire to raise children and spend time with siblings
- **Honor**, the desire for upright character
- **Idealism**, the desire for social justice
- **Independence**, the desire for self-reliance
- **Order**, the desire for structure
- **Physical Activity**, the desire for muscle exercise
- **Power**, the desire for influence or leadership

- **Romance,** the desire for beauty and sex
- **Saving,** the desire to collect
- **Social Contact,** the desire to have fun with peers
- **Status,** the desire for respect based on social standing
- **Tranquility,** the desire for safety
- **Vengeance,** the desire to confront provocations.

We all want the same 16 things: self-confidence, understanding, sustenance, family, character, justice, freedom, stability, muscle exercise, self-efficacy, sex, saving, belonging, respect, safety, and triumph.

COMPREHENSIVENESS OF 16 BASIC DESIRES

My colleagues and I believe that all psychologically important motives express one of the 16 basic desires or two or more of them acting in compound. Sensuality, for example, is motivated by a combination of two basic desires: romance and eating.

We think the list of 16 basic desires is comprehensive as is. It is possible that some revisions will be needed with future study, but we consider it unlikely that major additions will be needed. Although we don't expect significant future changes, we are open to modifications, provided they can be justified scientifically.

Our 16 basic desires are not self-explanatory. Indeed, we are often asked to explain why this or that motive appears to have been left out, and we typically reply by helping people understand how the motive in question is a variant or combination of the 16.

How does the desire to be wealthy fit into our schemata? Isn't the pursuit of money one of the most important motives driving the choices people make? Since wealth enhances social class, it falls under the basic desire for status.

What about creativity? Why is there no desire to be creative on the list of 16? Creativity is not included because it is not a universal goal shared by everyone. Many people do not aim to be creative, and some do not even value it. Remember the 16 basic desires is a list of universal goals common to everyone and deeply rooted in human nature.

Some evolutionary psychologists have wanted to know about the motives for survival and reproduction. The survival motive is included as the fear of death, which falls under the basic desire for tranquility. Further, the list of 16 basic desires includes motives essential for survival, such as eating, physical exercise, and cleanliness. The reproduction motive falls under the basic desire for romance/sex.

What about attention seeking? McDougall thought that attention-seeking falls under a self-display instinct that motivates people to show off, but I think it falls under the basic desire for status. We pay attention to people who are important while ignoring those who aren't.

I hope these illustrations clarify how I was thinking when I established my taxonomy of 16 basic desires, which is not based on personal opinions or experiences, but on statistical analysis of what many people told us.

NATURE VS. NURTURE

When people review the list of 16 basic desires for the first time, they have many questions. We are often asked, for example, whether or not the 16 basic desires have a genetic origin. We think they do because they have been demonstrated for people from three continents (North America, Europe, and Asia) and in multiple cultures. Further, a number of them can be observed in animals.

The 16 basic desires are valid across cultures. In a recent data analysis, we found very similar motivational profiles for 49,000 people from North America versus 8,000 people from Europe and Asia. The results of our surveys show that people living on Long Island, for example, are motivated by the same 16 basic desires that motivate people living in Singapore, Russia, South Africa, Mexico, India, Indonesia, Finland, or Germany.

Even if the desires have a genetic origin, as my colleagues and I suspect, culture and upbringing could play a significant role in determining the strength of each desire. Certain desires may be encouraged in some cultures or families and suppressed in others. Two teachers, for example, might encourage their children to start reading at a very early age, while two athletes might encourage sports participation. Parents in a small apartment might discourage uninhibited running around. Such differences in upbringing, especially in the early years, may strengthen or diminish the natural desires with which a child is born.

Culture and upbringing likely play significant roles in determining how people go about managing and gratifying their basic desires. People everywhere are motivated by hunger, power, curiosity, and so on, but they differ widely in the food they eat, how they go about satisfying their ambitions, and what they spend their time learning.

Another question many people ask us is whether or not the desires can be changed. Because our basic desires have a genetic origin, we tend to have the same basic needs and values throughout our lives. Curious children tend to become curious adolescents, who tend to become curious adults. Aggressive children tend to become aggressive adults (Eron & Huesmann, 1990).

Although we suspect that the basic desires usually change little throughout the adult years (see Reiss & Havercamp, 2005), people sometimes change how they satisfy them. A romantic person, for example, may change partners, a curious person might change topics of interest, or an athlete might change the preferred sports. Occasionally someone reports having changed their priorities after having found God. Nothing in my theory of 16 basic desires disputes such claims. I recognize the possibility that finding God, or even some lesser life event such as the death of a loved one, might change a person's priorities.

In summary, psychologists constructed many lists of psychological needs but none were scientifically valid. The 16 basic desires is the first list of psychological needs to meet scientific standards for reliability and validity. It is the only list based on what large numbers of people from diverse cultures say motivates them. It identifies the 16 motivating goals common to everyone and deeply rooted in human nature.

3

WHY PEOPLE EMBRACE RELIGION

Although everybody embraces all 16 basic desires, individuals differ in the strength of each desire. Typically, strong desires motivate individuals to seek frequent or intense experiences to satisfy the desire. A person with a strong need for power, for example, may go through everyday life seeking to experience a large quantity of power. Leadership roles, assertive behavior, and images of the divine as omnipotent all might appeal to people seeking to experience a large quantity of power. In contrast, weak desires motivate individuals to seek no more than infrequent or minimal experiences to satisfy the desire. A person with a weak need for power, for example, might go through everyday life avoiding most opportunities to experience power. Nonassertive behavior and religious submission to God both might appeal to people seeking to manage their experiences of power to low levels consistent with a weak need.

Average needs motivate individuals to seek moderate experiences. A person with an average need for power, for example, might tend to avoid both situations involving intense experiences with power and those involving intense experiences with submission. Or the individual might embrace power in one situation but avoid it in another. He or she might lead at work but follow at home.

The Reiss Motivation Profile® (RMP) is a standardized questionnaire that assesses which basic desires are strong, average, or weak for the individual who completes the questionnaire. In this chapter we will examine how the results of the RMP play out in the spiritual life of two people (one Christian and the other Jewish). Each individual completed the RMP and then was interviewed about his or her participation in religious activities. My intent was not a scientific study but simply to obtain an initial look at how religion might help the faithful satisfy their basic desires.

My hypothesis is that people are attracted to those aspects of religion that help them satisfy their strong and weak basic desires. A person with a strong basic desire for social contact, for example, might be attracted to religious festivals, while a person with a weak basic desire for social contact might be attracted to religious retreats. A person with a strong basic desire for vengeance might be attracted to jihad, but a person with a weak basic desire for vengeance might embrace forgiveness and gratitude. I assume that average basic desires can be gratified too easily and in too many ways to motivate people to embrace religion or any particular experience or gratification. The way my theory works, I pay little attention to average needs.

EMMA

Emma was a 63 year-old mother of two at the time of my interview. I consider her to be a religious person partially because she participates in church activities at least twice a week (and sometimes as often as four times a week), and she prays daily.

The results of Emma's RMP are summarized in Table 3-1. She has six strong desires, five weak desires, and five average desires. Her strongest desire is for family life. She values traditional morals (which is motivated by her strong need for honor) and is compassionate toward the poor and sick (which is motivated by her strong desire for idealism). She dislikes intellectually demanding activities (which is motivated by her weak desire for curiosity); she is a kind and gentle person (which falls under her weak basic desire for vengeance); and she is an unassuming person who puts on no airs (which is motivated by a weak basic desire for status).

Table 3-1
RMP Results for Emma, a Religious Christian

STRONG STRIVINGS	AVERAGE	WEAK STRIVINGS
Eating	Acceptance	Curiosity
Family	Independence	Physical Activity
Honor	Order	Power
Idealism	Romance	Status
Saving	Tranquility	Vengeance
Social Contact		

The meaning in Emma's life is centered on her family, and she turns to her religion to help fulfill this basic desire. When asked about her most vivid religious memories, Emma replied, "Being married in the church, having my children baptized in church, seeing my grandchildren in church and attending the same Sunday school that I attended." When asked why she believes God loves her, she responded, "God has given me a good husband, good children, good grandchildren, fairly good health, and good friends." Notice how her most vivid memories are about her family. She thinks of her church as a kind of family, saying, "We are all part of the church family, and having the same religion is a unifying force." She prays often for her family, and she has been blessed with healthy children and grandchildren.

Emma does not aspire to any leadership role in her church. This is consistent with her weak desire for power. She dislikes leadership roles generally, so she avoids such roles in her church.

Emma lives in an inexpensive rural area and struggles to make ends meet. Yet she is generous when it comes to charity. When an earthquake struck Haiti, she went to church, prayed for the victims, and donated money to the church's fund for Haitian victims. She turned to her religion to express her compassion (which is motivated by a strong desire for idealism).

Emma's parents were religious, and she is proud of them and of her Polish heritage. She eats ethnic foods and teaches her children ethnic songs. These beliefs and practices express her loyalty to her ancestors, which falls under her strong desire for honor. Further, she tries hard not to sin and believes she lives a basically moral life. She rejects the idea that God helps those who help themselves—this idea is associated with expedience (which is motivated by a weak need for honor)—but embraces the belief that God helps everyone (which is about not comparing people and thus expresses the value of a weak desire for vengeance).

Emma accepts the Bible as historical truth, believes in the Devil, and basically has a fundamentalist approach to religion. She says she does not meditate. These experiences are consistent with her weak desire for curiosity. She does not intellectually challenge what she has been taught about God and religion because she dislikes deep thought. The only notable disagreement she has with her religion is that she does not believe in the wrath of God (perhaps because of her weak desire for vengeance).

Emma satisfies her strong need for saving partially by collecting cards from funeral homes. "My favorite," she wrote, "is the Lord is my Shepherd prayer. I also collect rosaries."

In conclusion, Emma provides an example of a person for whom religion satisfies her most important basic desires and needs. Her life is centered on her family, as is her participation in her religion. Since she dislikes conflict and comparisons, she finds meaningful those aspects of her religion that teach her to embrace gentleness and reject anger and violence. From a psychological standpoint, her religion provides her with what she needs to fulfill her desires and to experience her life as meaningful.

Further, Emma is a good example of why it is invalid to say that the psychology of religion is about just one single all-important essence, such as the fear of death. Emma turns to her religion to satisfy her needs for parenting (which falls under the basic desire for family) and altruism (which falls under the basic desire for idealism). Psychometric science suggests that these needs are unrelated and have no common root. In the example of Emma, we see how religion is more than a belief or practice, but rather is a way of living.

TOM

Tom volunteered to complete the RMP, and without knowing the results, to be interviewed about his participation in his Jewish religion. At the time he was a 29 year-old married man with two daughters. He was a member of a temple located near his home in California, and he had a rabbinic ordination. He usually attended services daily, sometimes twice a day, and on Saturdays he spent much of his day in synagogue. Although he had no official duties in the synagogue, he sometimes was asked to deliver the sermon when the rabbi was away. The results of his RMP are summarized in Table 3-2.

Table 3-2

RMP Results for Tom, a Religious Jew

STRONG STRIVINGS	AVERAGE	WEAK STRIVINGS
Curiosity	Eating	Acceptance
Idealism	Family	Independence
	Honor	Order
	Physical Activity	Power
	Romance	Status
	Saving	Tranquility
	Social Contact	Vengeance

Freud and many social psychologists have argued that fear and anxiety, especially the fear of death, drives people like Tom to embrace religion. Religious people are afraid of dying, Freudians claim, but they don't know the extent of it, because some fears are unconscious. They look to God for protection, and they hope for an afterlife.

I disagree with the Freudian analysis of religion, with Tom being an excellent case in point. His low RMP score for tranquility suggests that he has significantly fewer fears and anxieties than most people do and, indeed, explains why he is a calm and relaxed person. His low RMP score for acceptance suggests he is self-confident. It doesn't make any sense that a calm, self-confident person like Tom would embrace religion to allay fears and anxiety. Is it possible that Tom is calm and relaxed because his faith allays his anxieties, including his fear of death? Is religion what makes him so calm? In a word, my answer is "no." Although anxious people may calm down at times and become less anxious, they do not become relaxed people. The predisposition to become anxious remains. Fearful people who turn to religion may become less anxious, but they remain more predisposed to anxiety and fear as compared with the average person.

The fear of death is just one of many diverse reasons why people embrace institutional religion. As suggested by his strong need for curiosity, Tom is an intellectual. He finds meaning in contemplation, ideas, and understanding. He turns to religion partially because it helps him contemplate the deeper meaning of life, which is a psychological motivator unrelated to the fear of death.

An anxious person wakes up most days looking for ways to relax and feel safe. In contrast, an intellectual like Tom wakes up each day thinking, analyzing, or strategizing. The anxious person goes through the day seeking safety; the intellectual goes through the day seeking understanding. They are simply different people with different interests and values.

Tom's intellectualism was evident not only from his high RMP score for curiosity but also from his thoughtful and analytical responses to the follow-up interview questions. His religion, he said, "appeals to both my rational and spiritual side." He reported interest in "proofs of the existence of God." At the university he enjoyed in-depth studies of Jewish law. He stated that part of what he likes best about his religion is studying Talmudic law and related medieval commentaries. One of his most vivid religious memories was, "Sitting in my rabbi's study, learning Talmud with him."

To an intellectual like Tom, contemplation, reflection, and understanding are meaningful activities. Ideas matter. Tom could have satisfied his needs in a wholly secular context by studying science, but he chose to embrace his religion for learning and understanding. Since he contemplated Jewish law as opposed to natural law, his religion imbued his intellectual activity with the added significance of divine relevance.

Because family is meaningful to Emma, she embraced religion to satisfy her family values. Because ideas are meaningful to Tom, he is attracted to the intellectual aspects of religion. Theology is of little interest to Emma, who had a low RMP score for curiosity, but it is important to Tom.

Tom's strong need for idealism implies a concern for the welfare of humanity. It motivates his charitable nature and his interest in helping others. "Within the Jewish community," he wrote, "I try to find opportunities to teach or lead services for those who may not have the same background I was afforded."

In his follow-up interview, Tom implied several times that his religion is about following God's commandments. The desire to follow commands falls under a weak need for power. Religion imbued his desire to be obedient with divine significance. Tom prays on a daily basis. A weak basic desire for independence motivates people to ask for help when they feel they need it.

Tom has a weak need for vengeance, which means he avoids conflict and finds meaning in peace and gentleness. When asked about the famous Bible passage of an eye for an eye, and a tooth for a tooth, he said it is about the importance of justice in a society. It is about a court's responsibility to exact justice; it is not a mandate for individual retaliation. Thus, he did not see the passage as justification for vengeance.

COMPOSITE MOTIVATION PROFILE OF RELIGIOUS PEOPLE

The examples of Emma and Tom show how the 16 basic desires play out in the lives of two religious individuals. They show how religion helps these people satisfy their individual psychological needs in meaningful ways.

We do not have to be religious in order to satisfy our needs, pursue our desires, and experience our lives as meaningful. Religious and secular organizations offer alternative lifestyles and activities for satisfying our needs. We have a need, for example, to educate our children. We can send them to public school or to religious school. Our children have a need for positive social experiences. We can encourage them to attend dances at a public school or at a church school. We have a need for altruism, which we can satisfy by giving to secular or religious charities.

Why do Emma and Tom turn to their religions to satisfy their needs? Why don't they rely instead on secular culture? Rather than turn to her church, Emma could satisfy her need for family life through secular activities such as camping, shopping, or vacationing together with her children and grandchildren. Tom could satisfy his intellectual needs by studying science or math.

Why do some people satisfy their needs through mostly religious activities while others do so through mostly secular activities? For some people it may depend on the cost of the activities. Perhaps it is less expensive and more affordable for many ordinary people to satisfy their needs religiously than through secular alternatives. If this is true, we should expect to find that poor people are more religious than are well-to-do people, and this apparently is the case (Miller, 2014).

Is there a particular desire profile associated with being religious? To explore this fascinating issue, we asked 558 adult Americans from diverse backgrounds to complete the RMP and to rate how religious they are: very, somewhat, or atheist (Reiss, 2000b). The four largest denominations represented in the sample were Catholic (n=171), Methodist (n=54), Baptist (n=44), and Presbyterian (n=44). The average age was 33 (range 18 to 83).

The results are presented in Table 3-3. The very religious Christians who participated in the study place above average valuation on family, honor (morality), idealism (charity), and order (ritual). They place below average valuation on independence,

Table 3-3
Composite RMP for Very Religious Christians

STRONG STRIVINGS	AVERAGE	WEAK STRIVINGS
Family	Acceptance	Independence
Honor	Curiosity	Romance
Idealism	Eating	Vengeance
Order	Physical Activity	
	Power	
	Saving	
	Social Contact	
	Status	
	Tranquility	

romance (sex), and vengeance. The study suggested that the basic desire for honor might be the single most important psychological motive of the religious people who participated in the study. Honor motivates loyalty to ancestors as well as character development. People with a strong need for honor are loyal, responsible, trustworthy, righteous, and self-disciplined. In contrast, those with a weak need for honor are expedient and opportunistic. The results imply that religion appeals to a significantly larger percentage of honorable people than to opportunists.

Vassilis Saroglou (2008, 2010) also reported that honor may motivate people to embrace Christianity. In a review of previously published studies, he concluded that religious people tend to have high scores on the Conscientious scale of the Big 5 personality test. This scale is roughly equivalent to the RMP scales for honor and idealism. On average, religious people have a stronger than average predisposition to behave morally and responsibly. Of course, there are many individual exceptions to this general finding.

Religion appeals to honorable people because it consistently supports their values. Religion helps people experience honor. It teaches morality to the young. It encourages worshipping a moral God and rejecting the Devil, who is pure evil. It praises the moral self-discipline of saints and ascetics. Further, religion is steeped in tradition and provides many reminders of ancestors (all of which fall under the basic desire for honor).

Religion offers experiences of honor that are too frequent or intense to appeal to expedient people who seek only some minimal degree of honor. Not wanting to be righteous, some expedient people may pride themselves on their skills for opportunism and promoting self-interest. Religion has nothing good to say about expedience, disloyalty to parents or ancestors, lying, and so on. Expedient people may turn to secular activities—finance, business, or sports—to satisfy their need for expedience (weak need for honor).

Church doctrines typically call for educating opportunistic people and turning them into people who behave righteously. As a psychologist, my own view is that changing people's desires and values is difficult to accomplish. I am not going to go so far as to suggest that religion cannot increase moral behavior by encouraging it, but for the most part expedient people change slowly if at all. There is little to motivate the change when people value expedience and take pride in opportunism. My view is that the vast majority of opportunistic adults aren't sincerely interested in changing their ways. Some are likely to ignore or shun institutional religion, which basically preaches they are wrong with respect to their expedient ways.

To put it simply, I think there are three categories of personality types with respect to the need for honor: honorable people, expedient people, and those who are sometimes honorable and sometimes expedient. Religion appeals to disproportionate numbers of honorable people because it expresses their values and helps them experience honor frequently and intensely.

Further, I think there are three categories of personality types with respect to the need for independence: independent people, interdependent people, and those who are sometimes independent and sometimes interdependent. Religion attracts interdependent people because they value connectedness and trust God to meet their needs. On the other hand, independent people place below-average value on interconnectedness. They do not wish to rely on anybody to meet their needs, not even on God. Independent-minded people may be uncomfortable with experiences of connectedness, including mysticism, because such experiences frustrate their need for a high degree of personal freedom.

The religious Christians in the Reiss (2000b) survey showed an above average need for family. Emma is an excellent example of this. Her religion offered many opportunities for her to satisfy her need for family life. Religion's support for family values is expressed by the saying, "The family that prays together, stays together."

Local Christian churches consistently preach the virtues of family values. They encourage young people to marry and to raise children within the faith. They offer social activities for families. In contrast, they offer very little support for those who want to remain single or for married couples who do not want to have children. Few religious stories or myths praise couples who choose not to have children.

The results of the Reiss (2000b) study also found that religious Christians placed a much lower value on confrontation and aggression, and a much higher value on cooperation and gentleness, than did the nonreligious Christians. This result is consistent with Christ's teaching to "turn the other cheek." Christianity strongly supports the values of gentle people, which suggests it might appeal to these individuals more than it does to aggressive people.

The motivation profile of the clergy may differ from that of the flock. In a survey of 49 Protestant seminary students, Havercamp and Reiss (2004) found a very high need for idealism. Apparently, the young Christian seminary students, all of whom were men, were motivated to join the seminary by the ideal of making the world a better place.

To summarize, the theory of 16 basic desires predicts a correspondence between a person's desire profile and his or her interests in religion. It implies that some individuals embrace religion to help them satisfy their desires, especially those that are strong or weak. Previous scholars may not have realized the extent to which religious beliefs and practices express basic desires because they did not have a reliable and valid tool for assessing basic desires. The

RMP may create new research opportunities for studying individuality and religious experiences.

IS SPIRITUALITY A SEVENTEENTH BASIC DESIRE?

My theory of 16 strivings for God does not recognize spirituality as a seventeenth basic desire. I believe that people relate to God through a comprehensive array of basic desires, not through a single mode of contact, or separate dimension of personality, called "spirituality." The 16 basic desires—the 16 dimensions of meaningful experience—connect the faithful to God through their basic desire for family when they sit down for a difficult conversation with a rebellious child. They are connected with God through their basic desire for honor when they care for their sick and aging parents. They are connected to God through their basic desire for intellectual stimulation when they are curled up in a chair reading philosophy. God is there for everyone who seeks him. He doesn't just work for the faithful when they meditate and pray. He inspires them 24/7.

Further, I disagree with those who say that people who pray, meditate, and attend church frequently are more spiritual than is anybody else. I reject spiritual elitism in favor of the view that everybody is equal before God. No matter how pious a person might or might not be, I believe that he or she is no closer to God than anybody else.

Religion is at its best when its message is inclusiveness of all kinds of people. The 16 basic desires is an inclusive construct equally applicable to all kinds of people. The construct of spirituality as a seventeenth basic desire is not an inclusive idea because it implies that some people are more spiritual than others.

Should the list of 16 basic desires be expanded to include spirituality as a seventeenth basic desire? My answer is negative, but other psychologists disagree with my view and are inclined to recognize spirituality as a seventeenth basic desire.

Ralph Peidmont (1999), a psychology professor at the University of Marymount Loyola, studies spirituality and personality. He constructed a new questionnaire, called ASPIRES (Piedmont, Werdekl, & Fernando, 2009), to assess how spiritual any individual might be. His aim is to measure spirituality objectively and then demonstrate scientifically that it is a distinct and separate dimension of personality. According to Piedmont, spiritual people believe life has a larger meaning and purpose, feel connected to a sacred reality, and value meditation or prayer. Future researchers might study the correlations between the ASPIRES and the RMP to learn the motives and values associated with spirituality.

In conclusion, it seems clear that the 16 basic desires play out in religion and spirituality. Future research is needed to evaluate whether or not spirituality should be recognized as a seventeenth basic desire. We also need to study in more detail the motivational forces that drive people to embrace religion.

4

GOD AS AN EXPRESSION OF OUR BASIC DESIRES

The late Stephen Judah was a marriage counselor who was active in local Christian groups in Columbus, Ohio. After reading my book *Who Am I* (Reiss, 2000a), he wanted to talk about how the 16 basic desires could be applied to marriage counseling. Over the course of the next year or so we did just that. I worked on conceptual issues while he counseled couples who had sought his help, applying what we had worked out. We created the Reiss Relationship Profile™ (RRP), which is an application of the Reiss Motivation Profile®.

It wasn't until two years later that Stephen asked me how the 16 basic desires played out in religion. I started to give Stephen an overview, saying that God's attributes are the greatest imaginable expression of 13 of the 16 basic desires. I started to say that the basic desire for acceptance motivates people to value salvation, the basic desire for curiosity motivates people to value omniscience, when Stephen's eyes lit up, and I knew I didn't have to say any more.

I was nonetheless struck by the fact that he failed to realize the connections between the 16 basic desires and God's attributes. If that vital relevance hadn't been clear to Stephen after two years of working with me, I realized it wouldn't necessarily be clear to anyone else either. It occurred to me that I should explicitly address the issue, which is what I intend to do here.

The Judeo-Christian God expresses the greatest, most perfect, most admirable qualities we can imagine. Saint Anselm (1033–1109), for example, defined God as, "that thing than which nothing more perfect can be thought..." (Armstrong, 1993, p. 132). He asked his readers to think of the greatest being that they could imagine or conceive—but then go on to reflect that God was even greater and more perfect than that.

Protestant theologian Rudolf Otto (1936) concluded, "We maintain, on the one hand... that the divine is indeed the highest, strongest, best, loveliest, and dearest that man can think of" (p. 166).

Now let's put these ideas together with the thesis of this book. On the one hand, our thesis is that human nature includes not one but 16 strivings for God. On the other hand, the Judeo-Christian image of God is intended as the greatest, most perfect, most admirable qualities we can imagine. It follows, then, that the attributes of God should be the greatest imaginable expression of the 16 basic desires. They are:

ACCEPTANCE AND A SAVIOR GOD

Then I saw a great white throne and him who was seated on it. From his presence earth and sky fled away, and no place was found for them. And I saw the dead, great and small, standing before the throne, and books were opened. Then another book was opened, which is the book of life. And the dead were judged by what was written in the books, according to what they had done. And the sea gave up the dead who were in it, Death and Hades gave up the dead who were in them, and they were judged, each one of them, according to what they had done. Then Death and Hades were thrown into the lake of fire. This is the second death, the lake of fire (Revelation 20:11-15).

The basic desire for acceptance motivates us to avoid rejection, failure, and criticism. Psychologically, it motivates interest in the religious concept of Judgment. Some religions teach that God will sit in judgment of us. He will consider everything about us and render a final judgment of salvation versus damnation. If we are saved, we go to heaven and experience eternal bliss. If we are damned, we go to hell and experience eternal agony.

From a psychological perspective, salvation is the greatest imaginable act of acceptance. It trumps all other experiences of acceptance, rejection, criticism, and praise. When your boss criticizes you, for example, you can find comfort in your belief that, in the end, what matters is your relationship with God, not with your boss. When your boyfriend or girlfriend rejects you, you can find comfort in your faith that God accepts you. No matter how you spend your time on this Earth—rich or poor, good-looking or disfigured, healthy or ill—it all pales in significance as compared to God's final judgment.

The idea of God's judgment goes all the way back to ancient Egypt where Osiris, the god of the underworld, was believed to sit in judgment of the dead, or at least those who managed to find him. The Egyptian priests taught that Osiris weighed the deceased's heart against a feather, the symbol of truth. If the heart were heavier, the deceased would immediately be consumed by monsters or dropped into a fiery pit. If the feather were heavier, the deceased would be permitted to continue on into the Kingdom of the Dead.

The ancient Persian religion founded by Zoroaster also recognized a Day of Judgment, as did the doomsayers of the Jewish faith. This latter group—common at the time of the historical Jesus—taught that God would resurrect the dead and then judge each and every person who ever lived, saving the righteous and damning the wicked. Similarly, modern Catholicism teaches that God judges each of us upon our death, saving some for the blissful Kingdom of God, while damning others to the fires of Hell. From a psychological standpoint, the Day of Judgment can be viewed as the greatest imaginable source of evaluation anxiety. No test at school, no job evaluation, is riskier or has higher stakes. God either accepts or rejects us for all Eternity. He never changes his mind or even reconsiders. There is no appeal and no second chance.

The religious image of God-as-Savior imbues the basic desire for acceptance with eternal significance. It teaches the faithful to find meaning in judgment, favorable evaluation, self-confidence, and optimism. The human psyche reasons that, " If God saves me, I must be worthy, regardless of my failures or what anybody else says. If God values me, I should value myself."

When we think God accepts us, we find confidence and are ready to take on the world. Norman Vincent Peale (1956) provided examples of people who gained their self-confidence through faith in God's love for them.

On the other hand, those who are not religious—or who doubt God as savior—will still find the pursuit of acceptance from parents and loved ones to be deeply meaningful. Should this need be frustrated rather than gratified, however, they won't have a fallback like religion to help satisfy that need and get them back on their feet. In a difficult divorce, for example, some people are devastated, and with their need for acceptance frustrated, may begin to doubt their self-worth and the meaningfulness of their lives. If they are religious, they may turn to God for a sense of basic acceptance.

In conclusion, the concept of God's judgment imbues the basic desire for acceptance with additional meaning implied by the possibilities of salvation and damnation. Being saved by God may become an overarching purpose in life, at least for some people of faith. Even in a religion that teaches there is nothing one can do to affect God's judgment, the faithful still hope otherwise.

CURIOSITY AND AN OMNISCIENT GOD

His understanding has no limit (Psalms 147:5).

Intellectual curiosity, which is one of the 16 basic desires, is a need for understanding associated with the emotion of wonder. The desire to understand gives purpose and meaning to intellectual activities. It motivates us to value ideas and wisdom. Humans are curious about numerous topics—everything from practical issues, such as how best to grow crops, to philosophical matters, such as who are we and how were we created.

Religions have connected the basic human desire for curiosity to God in a number of different ways. Christians, Hindus, Muslims, and Jews worship God as omniscient or all-knowing. Since one cannot know more than everything, omniscience is the greatest imaginable satisfaction of the basic desire for curiosity.

God's omniscience imbues intellectual activities with divine significance. Human knowledge is infinitesimal in comparison to what God knows. Still the more we learn, the more God-like we become. If God is omniscient, we reason, then knowledge is good, and the pursuit of knowledge is a worthy and meaningful goal.

The conception of God as infinite wisdom and truth inspires religious intellectuals and adds meaning to their search for truth. God is the infallible source of all truth. As St. Augustine (1964/397) put it in his *Confessions,* "Where I have found truth, there I have found my God, the truth itself." God is infinitely wise and possesses unsurpassed powers of reasoning. He adds purpose to those who seek truth.

Aristotle (1953/330 B.C.E.) imagined God as pure thought. He reasoned that God thinks only about that which is perfect, namely, himself. He does not know about the physical world, even though his thought had set it in motion. Aristotle imagined God as an eternal, indivisible, unmovable, and spiritual being. Other philosophers imagined God as pure reason—reason itself, and the logic governing the universe including the movement of the planets. He is the controlling intelligence in the universe and is the ultimate explanation of everything that happens. In conclusion, the basic desire for curiosity motivates us to value God as omniscient and the ultimate source of truth.

FAMILY—GOD AS FATHER

And I will be a father to you, and you shall be sons and daughters to me, says the Lord Almighty (2 Corinthians 6:18).

The basic desire for family motivates young couples to have children, raise them, and love them. It also motivates people to care about siblings. It is among the most meaningful experiences in the lives of many people.

Please note that parents' love for their children—and children's love for their parents—are motivated by different basic desires. A parent's love for the child falls under what we call the basic desire for family, while the child's love for the parent is motivated by what we call the basic desire for honor. We need two basic desires to analyze the parent-child relationship because adults may love their children much more than they love their own parents, or vice versa. Mahatma Gandhi, for example, was devoted to his father but showed noticeably less devotion to his children. When his father became deathly ill, Gandhi dropped out of school to take care of him. After his father passed away, Gandhi left his wife and children behind in India while he studied law in England.

I contend that parental love is the greatest imaginable expression of our basic desire for family. Families spend time together, have fun together, help support each other, but it is the love a parent experiences that most completely expresses the warmth of family life.

God's parental nature is revealed in the Christian Trinity. Christians believe that God loves us as a father loves his children. He loves us so much he sent his only Son to Earth to save us. Jews also worship God as a parental figure.

God's love is conceived as the greatest imaginable love because of its infinite purity and all-encompassing quality. His love inspires parents to love their children as God loves them. Estelle, a very religious mother and grandmother I knew personally, often would say that she tried to love her daughter and grandchildren as she was taught that God loved her.

At times when children become difficult or perhaps even rebel and yell at us, religious parents find strength in knowing that their mission from God is to love their children as he loves them. Priests and rabbis counsel troubled parents when challenges arise, and churches encourage the faithful to marry, multiply, and to stay together by loving each other and by worshiping together as a family.

In conclusion, the basic desire for family is the psychological force that motivates us to think of God in family terms by conceiving of him as the father and as the son. This gives added purpose and significance to parenting.

HONOR—GOD AS PERFECT GOODNESS

How great is Thy goodness, which Thou hast stored up for those who fear Thee, which Thou hast wrought for those who take refuge in Thee, before the sons of men (Psalms 31:19)!

The basic desire for honor has a number of crucial aims, the most important being adherence to a moral code of conduct. Instead of acting out of self-interest, the honorable person conforms his or her behavior to a moral code. The honorable person keeps promises, behaves in a responsible manner, and is trustworthy. The opposite of honor is expedience, which is acting out of self-interest when opportunity arises.

The other aims of this basic desire are to be respected based on one's character and to be loyal to one's parents and ancestors. Perhaps the most common way the faithful express loyalty to their parents is to behave morally while embracing their parents' religion and culture. When children from a religious family grow up and marry within their faith, for example, they are honoring their heritage by embracing it.

I contend that God is the greatest imaginable expression of the basic desire for honor because perfect goodness is one of his attributes. Further, he is the moral lawgiver. On Mt. Sinai God gave Moses the Ten Commandments, which became the basis for numerous moral codes in Western societies. Killing and stealing, for example, are regarded as immoral most everywhere. God also opposes the ultimate source of evil, the Devil himself.

We do not merely honor God: We worship him. There is no respect humans can pay that is greater than that expressed in worshipping God. No one is more honorable than God.

Many scholars—both those of faith and those who are atheists—have wondered how it is possible for a God of infinite goodness to tolerate evil. If God is infinitely good, omniscient, and infinitely powerful, he would know beforehand when evil is about to strike and would not let it happen. Why then did God not stop Hitler from murdering millions of Jews in the Holocaust? Why does he tolerate cancer and other diseases rather than putting an end to them? Such questions are so common philosophers even have an expression for them: the "Problem of Evil."

The "Problem of Evil" is an important theological puzzle, but the underlying psychology may be less paradoxical. I think we conceive of God as perfectly good because this attribute is the greatest imaginable expression of the basic desire for honor; as infinitely knowledgeable because this attribute is the greatest imaginable expression of the basic desire for curiosity; and as infinitely powerful because this attribute is the greatest imaginable expression of the basic desire for power. These three desires—honor, curiosity, and power—are *psychologically* compatible, and they all can be experienced as meaningful at the same time. There is no psychological contradiction in saying that we conceive of God as perfect goodness, omniscient, and omnipotent. The three psychological forces are driving a logical contradiction, but as I discuss in Chapter 7 there are other examples of this in religious dogma.

The Judeo-Christian conception of God imbues moral behavior, self-discipline, and character with additional meaning.

When the faithful behave morally, they not only are doing what is right but also are honoring God. By embracing the Ten Commandments, the Judeo-Christian faithful feel closer to God.

IDEALISM—GOD AS COMPASSION/ PERFECT SOCIAL JUSTICE

Blessed is he that considereth the poor: the Lord will deliver him in time of trouble. The Lord will preserve him, and keep him alive; and he shall be blessed upon the earth: and thou wilt not deliver him unto the will of his enemies (Psalms 41:1-2).

Idealism motivates compassion, acts of charity, and acts of social justice. We feel outrage when our need for idealism (sense of social justice) is frustrated. Whereas the basic desire for honor motivates loyalty to one's ethnic or religious group, the basic desire for idealism—such as helping the needy, the poor, the ill, or the downtrodden—motivates loyalty to humanity as a whole.

Idealism is the primary motive for selflessly helping others, but it is not the only one. Personal sacrifice out of friendship falls under the basic desire for social contact. Sacrificing for our children falls under the basic desire for family. Sacrificing for our parents falls under the basic desire for honor. None of these acts is considered to be a true example of idealism because the aims are friendship, family, and honor. With true idealism, the intention is social justice, fairness, and/or selflessly assisting the community as a whole. Idealism motivates us to help people we don't know simply because they are human beings.

The Christian God is a champion of the downtrodden who sides with the weak and the oppressed. He is the greatest imaginable advocate for the needy. He alone has the power and resources to lift all from poverty, reverse the devastating effects of illness, and bring about everlasting world peace. Jesus reminded his followers that God gave life to their fellow human beings, so they, too, should care about them.

The conception of God as champion of the poor, the sick, the disadvantaged, and the beaten down gives increased meaning to acts of charity—sometimes called "God's work." "In all three faiths [Judaism, Christianity, and Islam]," Karen Armstrong (1993) observed, "He [God] has inspired an ideal of social justice" (p. 20). According to my theory, God's interest in the downtrodden appeals primarily to people with a strong desire for idealism because these individuals typically seek frequent and intense experiences of compassion.

INDEPENDENCE—
GOD AS SELF-SUFFICIENT REALITY

And God said unto Moses, I AM THAT I AM...(Exodus 3:14).

The basic desire for independence motivates us to make our own way in life without asking for assistance or favors from others, to make our own decisions, and to do things our way. We experience the joy of personal freedom when we are self-reliant, but we experience feelings of dependency when we are not.

The primal roots of this basic desire may be the same instincts that drive animals to leave the nest and set out on their own, thus increasing the territory over which food is sought and giving the species a better chance of survival. The desire for independence prods adolescents to set out from their parents' home and make homes of their own. As children go out into the world to pursue their education or careers, they may move to another city or just across town. But most do set out from their family and succeed in supporting themselves on their own.

The basic desire for independence motivates us to value God's self-sufficient nature. The Judeo-Christian God requires nothing from any source other than himself to express his will. Pure spirit, he can exist without anyone or anything else. He doesn't need oxygen, food, or water. He doesn't need money, and he doesn't need friends. "I am that I am," as he told Moses in the ultimate statement of independent existence. Philosophers have described God as "absolutely self-sufficient," as "absolute freedom," as "reality," as "true existence," and as "being."

God's independence inspires the faithful to imitate him by taking care of themselves and by making their own decisions. It encourages independent-minded people to view freedom as God-given and as the natural state of humankind. As the saying goes, "God helps those who help themselves."

Although the Judeo-Christian conception of God as self-sufficient expresses values motivated by the basic desire for independence, the Hindu conception of God as ever-present (being, reality itself, consciousness) expresses the value of interconnectedness. Independence and interconnectedness are opposite values. Mystical conceptions of an unseen reality also express the value of interconnectedness. In the theory of 16 strivings for God, a low or weak need for independence motivates people to value interconnectedness. People with a high or strong need for independence should find meaning in deities that need nothing to be; those with a low or weak need should find meaning in mystical visions of the Absolute.

ORDER—GOD AS ETERNAL ORDER

"For I know the plans I have for you," declares the LORD... (Jeremiah 29:11).

The basic desire for order has a number of aims, the most important of which is structure, but also sameness and cleanliness. Rituals, scheduling, planning, organizing, and cleaning are all activities we undertake in the interest of this basic desire. Cleanliness, of course, has survival value because it prevents disease. When our need for order is met, we feel comfortable and secure. When it is frustrated, we feel uncomfortable and anxious.

The opposite of order is chaos, formlessness, spontaneity, and flux. While some people intrinsically value formlessness and spontaneity, nobody values chaos. Human beings typically experience flux and continual change as meaningless. For the faithful this is where the eternal and immutable God comes in. You may lose all your money in an economic recession; you may lose your health to disease; or you may lose loved ones to accident or war. Your house could be leveled in a tornado, and your city could be destroyed in a hurricane. Yet there will always be God, and he will always be the same. It is the basic desire for order that makes such thoughts comforting.

The ancient Babylonian poem "Enuma Elish" described creation as the imposition of form on a sloppy mess where everything lacked boundary. The first words of the Bible tell us that in the beginning the earth was without form. God imposed order by separating light from darkness, day from night, firmament from water, and so on.

Religion teaches that God has a divine plan for each of us. We may not know what his plan is, but we can be sure he has one. The plan gives purpose and meaning to our lives. It implies that everything that happens to us and around us, no matter how insignificant it may seem, happens for a reason and that reason is part of a plan known to God.

God is conceived of as the eternal order of the universe. In his influential 1802 book *Natural Theology,* William Paley asserted that the orderliness and detail of the body reveal the work of a Creator because the adaptations of the various parts to each other were very unlikely to have happened by chance alone. This view is known as the "design argument" for the existence of God. Although Richard Dawkins among others has disputed such arguments, the orderliness of the universe remains for many a powerful source of comfort.

According to my theory, orderliness and cleanliness are psychologically related, and both attract people with high order to embrace religious rituals. The faithful sense a purer spirit when they are clean. They feel they are living as God intended to them to live. All major religions teach that cleanliness is next to godliness. The Koran says explicitly that God loves cleanliness. While everything in the universe can become contaminated, God does not have any impurities whatsoever.

The Hindu Trimurti refers to the three aspects or forms of the Divine overseeing the process of birth–death–rebirth. Brahma is the deity who creates the universe and everything in it; Vishnu preserves and protects; and Shiva destroys and transforms. The process as a whole expresses the value of order because it is recurrent, eternal, and always occurs in the same sequence. Further, Vishnu expresses the values of people with a high need for order, while Shiva, an agent of change, expresses the values of people with a low need for order.

PHYSICAL ACTIVITY—GOD AS ALMIGHTY

He that dwells in the shelter of the Most High shall abide under the shadow of the Almighty (Psalms 91:1).

This basic desire motivates physical exercise and muscle movement. It motivates people to value fitness and to participate in sports. It is a survival need because muscles decay without physical activity, threatening health. People experience vitality when this basic desire is satisfied, but they feel restless when it is frustrated.

The conception of God as almighty is the greatest imaginable expression of the human aim for physical strength. God lifts mountains; people strive to lift weights. God does not get tired; people strive for endurance in a marathon. He is a force stronger than any army or act of nature. It may seem like a bit of a stretch to suggest that the Judeo-Christian God is the greatest imaginable expression of the basic desire for physical activity. Although God is conceived as almighty, unlike the Homeric deities, the Judeo-Christian deity has no body, does not have muscles, and the concepts of fitness and wellness can't be applied to him. Nevertheless, God's strength, though not arising from muscle fitness, is physically expressed, as when he parted the sea for the Hebrews to pass and then crushed the Egyptian army that attempted to follow. Further, God has imbued human beings, notably Samson, with muscle strength.

The faithful are comforted by God's strength. When the faithful imagine that God is with them, they think the mightiest force in

the universe is their ally. This imbues the desire to be strong for
with the additional significance of imitating the divine, even
though we are infinitely less powerful. It motivates the faithful to
take care of their body.

POWER—GOD AS CREATOR AND LORD

*By the word of the LORD the heavens were made, And by
the breath of His mouth all their host. He gathers the waters
of the sea together as a heap; He lays up the deeps in store-
houses. Let all the earth fear the LORD; Let all the
inhabitants of the world stand in awe of Him. For He spoke,
and it was done; He commanded, and it stood fast (Psalms
33:6–12).*

The basic desire for power is about assertion of will, which can
make itself felt in many forms: leadership, achievement, ambition,
and wanting to be in control of other people. When we can fulfill
our need for power, we experience the joy of self-efficacy. When
we are unable to satisfy our need for power, we may experience
frustration or even humiliation. Power has survival benefits for
animals in the wild because the dominant animal pushes the others
from food and eats first. Dominant animals also have their choice
of mates.

The psychoanalyst Alfred Adler (1964/1927) thought that
power was the overarching psychological force driving the human
psyche. He believed that infants and children acquire unconscious
feelings of inferiority by comparing themselves to their bigger, more
powerful parents. He thought that adolescents and adults strive for
superior power to compensate for these old feelings. Adler's striving
for superiority falls under the basic desire for power.

The Judeo-Christian God is the ultimate expression of power.
His interventions in human life express his power or "grace," as
when he healed the sick. He is *the* Lord—the greatest imaginable
leader—who rules over all of nature, from the motion of the planets

to the building of anthills. But having established the order of nature, he also can override that order at will. We call God's interventions in what we consider the laws of nature "miracles."

God is a force so powerful he can do anything at all including creating the universe itself. *There is no greater achievement imaginable than creation.*

The faithful find meaning in God's power. Their own impulses to lead or achieve are validated by God's example. The faithful reason (and indeed theologians have supported this thinking) that since God has will, our own will is godlike even though it is nothing compared with his.

SOCIAL CONTACT—GOD AS A FRIEND

You are my friends if you do what I command you. No longer do I call you servants, for the servant does not know what his master is doing; but I have called you friends, for all that I have heard from my Father I have made known to you (John 15:14-15).

The basic desire for social contact motivates us to make friends, join groups, and have fun. It may have evolved because of the safety found in numbers when primates played together and were less attentive to the possible approach of prey.

God sometimes is presented as a friend. The Bible says that Abraham was called "the friend of God" (James 2:23). A well-known Christian hymn suggests "we have a friend in Jesus."

According to psychologist James Pratt (1921), many people conceive of God as their friend and look to him for social support and fellowship. The faithful talk to God in their heads and describe him as friendly. They also view his messengers—angels—as friendly.

Friendship with God is different from friendship with other people. According to the theory of 16 basic desires, people with a strong need for friends typically like to socialize, have fun, joke around, and party. This quality does not apply to friendship with God. Furthermore, we smile, show interest, and offer help to friends, but these behaviors also do not apply to our relationship with God.

STATUS—GOD AS DIVINITY

King of kings, and Lord of lords (Revelation 19:16).

The aim of this basic desire is respect based on social standing. It motivates people to seek high social class, high birth, wealth, and popularity. When we fulfill our need for status, we feel important, and perhaps even superior. When this need goes unfulfilled, we feel insignificant and perhaps even inferior.

The primal root of this basic desire is the need for attention. Newborn animals of all kinds get their parents to address their needs by calling attention to themselves. The primal connection between attention seeking and status is reflected in the habits of upwardly mobile individuals, who seek the attention of people with high social standing but not those who appear to them to be unimportant. Further, status can lead to privilege during times of emergency. When the Titanic was sinking, for example, it was the upper-class passengers who had first access to the lifeboats.

In monarchies, the sovereign is the person of greatest status in that country and usually is regarded as the head of high society. Below the sovereign come princes and princesses, followed by other royals such as dukes and duchesses. Social class for non-royals is based largely on wealth, which determines where one lives, how one dresses, and so on. In the Hindu caste system, it is the priests, scholars, and philosophers who occupy the highest social class.

God has the greatest imaginable status because he sits on the throne of the universe. He is the sovereign above all sovereigns. Even kings recognize this, often ascribing their own right to rule to God's appointment of them.

Divinity is the highest imaginable status partially because it is associated with the exalted qualities of immortality, infinite nature, transcendence, and pure spiritual existence. No human being can aspire to divine status since no human being can achieve these exalted qualities.

The faithful find meaning in God's divine status. Some may consider themselves important simply because they were created by God, especially in the image of God.

TRANQUILITY—GOD AS PROTECTOR

I am thy shield (Genesis 15:1).

The basic desire for tranquility motivates avoidance of fear and pain. Its primal origins are in animal instincts to flee danger and seek safety. When this desire is satisfied, we feel relaxed and serene. When it is frustrated, we are frightened and anxious.

The Judeo-Christian God is infinitely serene because he has nothing to fear or worry about. He is not afraid of dying. He does not worry about financial troubles. He isn't afraid of the Devil. The emotions of fear and anxiety do not apply to him.

The faithful consider God as the greatest imaginable protector and, thus, as a source of emotional calm. They manage their fears by thinking God is on their side. God is often portrayed as a fatherly figure who looks after us from heaven and who may intervene to protect us when we most need him. He can heal the sick, raise the dead, and strike down enemies. He commands the forces of nature including the seas, the weather, the cycles of disease, the mountains, and the sky.

According to my theory, Freudian psychologists have greatly exaggerated the significance of anxiety and fear in religion. Some people turn to God to protect them from death and danger, but safety is not the ultimate goal of life. I know many chronically ill people who face a significant risk of death without embracing religion. Some just tolerate the anxiety.

VENGEANCE—THE WRATH OF GOD

Let no man deceive you with vain words: for because of these
things cometh the wrath of God upon the children of disobe-
dience (Ephesians 5:6).

Vengeance is one of the 16 basic desires of human nature. The primal provocations are threats to status, threats to territory, invasion of personal space, threats to our children, competition for resources, access to potential mates, strange or unfamiliar people, and aggressive or unfriendly behavior by others.

The desire for vengeance is yet another quality that we see in the God of the Bible, especially the Hebrew Bible, where God is angered by disloyalty, idolatry, disobedience, and sin. We can imagine no greater anger than the wrath that flooded the world and later destroyed Sodom and Gomorrah, punishing humanity for its wickedness. Some Jews have viewed their misfortunes over the centuries—invasion, enslavement, displacement, and holocaust—as punishment from God.

The basic desire for vengeance motivated religious wars, persecutions, and inquisitions. Historically, many wars have been fought over religion. Pope Bernard, for example, told the second crusaders to show their love for Christ by slaughtering Muslims and hacking them to death. Japanese kamikaze pilots believed that God sanctioned their suicidal missions to kill Americans, who at the time of attack might have been praying to God to destroy the Japanese military.

In earlier civilizations, people worshipped deities or war gods that were thought to have the capacity to facilitate military victory. In her book *A History of God,* Karen Armstrong (1993) wrote that the conception of YHWH began as a Jewish tribal deity who had proved his worth in war long before he became the one and only God of the Jews.

At first blush, the depictions of God's terrifying wrath might seem to be a thinly disguised effort on the part of those who wrote the Bible to scare people into obedience. The average person is told, "Turn to God or his wrath will be aroused against you." I suggest, however, that there is a deeper message at play here: God's wrath validates the confrontational impulse within competitive or aggressive individuals. The religious warrior goes into battle thinking that since God is on his side the results have meaning beyond life and death.

THE THREE REMAINING DESIRES

The remaining three basic desires—romance, eating, and saving—are not attributes of the Judeo-Christian God. We will consider each very briefly.

ROMANCE

Some religions, notably Hinduism, have male and female gods, but Judaism and Christianity do not. God is not viewed as married; there is no Mrs. God. The Judeo-Christian God has no body and is not conceived of as a sexual being.

EATING

Since the Judeo-Christian God is pure spirit, he has no body and does not eat. He is not presented as the greatest imaginable eater. That said, religion teaches that God gives us our food. Religious dietary laws tell the faithful how God wants them to eat. For the faithful, meals not only satisfy their need for nourishment but also can take on the added significance of obedience to God.

SAVING

Saving is to collect or hoard in preparation for the future. God has no need to prepare for the future and, thus, he is not conceived of as the greatest imaginable saver.

GODS AS PROJECTIONS OF BASIC DESIRES

The idea that God is a projection of human desires has long been associated with atheism. Ludwig Feuerbach (1964/1841), for example, believed that God is merely a projection of the human mind and, thus, not real. Humans don't discover God, he wrote, but rather create him. Feuerbach's evidence is that people worship gods who have human qualities. He implies that if God really exists, we would not conceive of him in human terms.

Feuerbach observed that many gods have human qualities, not just the Judeo-Christian deity. The Homeric gods, for example, eat, drink, and have children. As noted already, the Hindu gods make love.

So what are we to make of the correspondence between human nature and the qualities we attribute to the gods? According to Feuerbach, it means that God is just an invention of the human psyche with no independent existence. He wrote that, "Man's belief in god is nothing other than his belief in himself... in his god he reveres and loves nothing other than his own being (Feuerbach (1964/1841, p. 182). "By his God thou knowest the man" (Feuerbach, 1964/1841, p. 175).

Feuerbach's unstated assumption is that we would know of a "real" God through our senses and not our psyche. We would "look," so to speak, see he is God, and the qualities we perceive when we look would not be human qualities. The flaw in this analysis is that the faithful do not conceive of God as a material object. They cannot see him with their eyes or hear him with their ears. Instead they look within themselves, discover what is meaningful in life, and then conceive of God as the greatest imaginable expression of meaning.

Stardate 3468. A fantastically powerful energy field has suddenly halted the starship USS Enterprise. Captain James T. Kirk orders his crew to free the Enterprise, but nothing they try works. Television viewers across America wonder what force could be so strong as to render the pride of Starfleet motionless in space. Even Spock, the famed science officer with pointed ears, cannot figure out how to free the Enterprise. Having gone where no man had gone before, the crew of the USS Enterprise encounters something very unusual. Amazingly the Greek god Adonis appears and addresses the Enterprise crew as his "beloved children." Holy cow! The Star Trek crew has discovered Mt. Olympus, the mythical home of Greek gods.

Do you believe that some future starship might encounter God in a faraway region of the universe? Is that what religion is all about, worshipping a god who lives "up there" and watches over us? Were the mythical gods of the ancient world—such as Adonis, Jupiter, and Ra—space travelers (or as the History Channel on cable television calls them, "ancient aliens") who visited Earth centuries ago? Did the unsophisticated Earth people mistake these scientifically advanced visitors for gods? These are intriguing ideas, although I personally don't put much stock in them.

Our image of God is affected by a projection of our basic desires, but I don't see how this supports atheism. If you accept, as I do, the idea that God is not of this world and that he does not live in the sky, then how could we possibly know of him except through our deepest desires, and most meaningful experiences?

In conclusion, the 16 basic desires are connected to the Judeo-Christian conception of God, with at least 13 of them so strongly connected that their most profound expressions are divine attributes. This observation doesn't support atheism but instead interprets God as an expression of universally admired qualities, such as savior, wise, powerful, and protector. If our concept of God did not express our deepest desires and needs, he would be meaningless to us.

In suggesting how our image of God is connected to our basic desires, I am not embracing atheistic ideas of God as nothing more than a projection of human desire, nor am I saying that God has no independent existence apart from how we imagine him. I am talking about how people come to a connection with God. My comments, therefore, have no theological implications. They concern rather the psychology of religious experiences. From this vantage, I am exploring the nexus between human nature and faith. I am pointing out that the human conception of God is an expression of what is most meaningful to us. The only logical alternative would be to conceive of God as meaningless, which would be absurd.

The Swiss psychologist Carl Jung (1960) argued that our image of God must be rooted in human nature or we would be incapable of experiencing the divine as meaningful. We must connect psychological factors—such as our deepest values—to our perception of God or we would experience him as just another object. He argued that God is found by looking within the soul, not to the heavens. Sky gods are objects of doubtful meaningfulness to us, he asserted, but the God accessed through our soul is experienced as the ground of all Being.

Jung (1960, 1933, 1923) rejected the view that it smacks of blasphemy to connect psychological factors to the divine. He suggested that we all inherit an idea of God through that part of the psyche he called the collective unconscious. According to Jung, the question of whether or not God exists and actually planted an idea of himself in our unconscious is a theological question. The role of the psychologist is to explore our unconscious idea of God and to describe how the conscious mind accesses this idea.

Freud and Jung were two psychologists who studied the unconscious meaning of religion. In this book I am exploring how consciously held values are expressed in religion. I am challenging the idea that what is meaningful and deep is unconscious, in favor of the idea that what is meaningful and deep is universal.

5

WHAT MOTIVATES ASCETICISM?

We are exploring the connections between the 16 basic desires of human nature and religion. Thus far we have learned how the 16 basic desires might help individuals discover why they embrace certain aspects of religion but not others. We also have learned that the Judeo-Christian God is conceived of as the greatest imaginable expression of 13 basic desires. In total, this is substantial evidence that Judeo-Christian religions carefully address the 16 basic desires.

We now consider how the 16 basic desires might help us understand asceticism, which is an austere lifestyle devoted to worshipping the divine. Although monks and nuns provide the most common examples of this lifestyle, certain ascetic practices such as fasting and celibacy are incorporated in modern religion. Catholic priests, for example, are celibate. On their Day of Atonement, Jews fast from sunset to sunset and spend their time in worship and prayer. Buddhist monks and nuns who follow the Vinaya rules deny themselves food each day after lunch.

Important religious figures embraced ascetic practices. Moses, for example, fasted for 40 days and nights to purify himself to receive the Ten Commandments. Jesus, too, fasted for 40 days and nights. Siddhartha Gautama, the founder of Buddhism, was born into a wealthy family, but his comfortable lifestyle did not satisfy his inner need for meaning. He lost interest in worldly pleasures, renounced his wealth, and left his home to join a band of ascetics in the forest. Eventually, however, he decided that mortification is not the true path to the divine.

BRIEF CASE EXAMPLES OF ASCETICS

Let's take a quick look at the features of the ascetic lifestyle by briefly considering some of the individuals who became famous for practicing it. History has recorded many examples of religious people who cultivated ascetic hardships. Typically they renounced all ambitions, dressed plainly, and denied themselves amusements such as dancing and parties. Some left their home and possessions to live in forests, caves, deserts, mountains, or other solitary places. Some broke family ties and lived alone in "cells," which are small, restricted areas. Some carried weights, cut their bodies, or endured the discomfort of sitting on hard chairs without cushions.

Saint John Vianney, for example, was a French country priest who pursued holiness by embracing discomfort and hardship. As described by James (1918/1890), "[Vianney] imposed it on himself that he should never smell a flower, never drink when parched with thirst, never drive away a fly... never sit down, never lean upon his elbows when he was kneeling" (p. 266).

Antony founded a monastic way praised by Martin Luther for being true to the spirit of the gospel. Born in Egypt in 251, he left his home at 19 shortly after his parents died. He lived in the desert in complete solitude. When he was alone in the wilderness, he sometimes experienced carnal desires, which he attributed to the devil's trying to tempt him. Mindful of the possibility of eternal damnation should he relieve his sexual tensions, Antony remained celibate by staying true to Christ's love and by showing the devil the cross.

Antony embraced a number ascetic practices. He chose to live in the wilderness where opportunities to socialize were minimal to nonexistent. He sold his property and embraced a life of poverty. He denied and resisted his sexual needs. He devoted his days to prayer.

Blessed Beatrice of Nazareth, a Flemish Cistercian nun, practiced asceticism. She was born into a well-to-do family in 1200 as the youngest of six children and died 68 years later as the first prioress of the Abbey of Our Lady of Nazareth in Belgium. Her ascetic practices included fasting, whipping her body with sharply-pointed thorn branches, exposing herself to cold, and excessively reciting prayers such as the Psalter of the Blessed Virgin. In order to strengthen self-control through practice, she cut and bruised much of her body by putting yew branches on her bed. At times she slept on a stone or a piece of wood instead of a bed with a pillow. These practices began in secret in her pre-teen years and took on a ritualistic quality. They were disapproved by her superiors who required her to curtail them, which she did to some extent.

Saint Benedict, who became one of the Catholic Church's most influential figures regarding monastic life, practiced asceticism. Whereas Antony lived in solitude in a cave, Benedict lived at times in communal retreats. He wrote the *Rule,* a manual that spells out the duties of monks and the organization of monastic life. For 15 centuries, the *Rule* of Saint Benedict was an influential guide for life within Christian monasteries. The *Rule* calls for prayer, obedience to the divine, humility, simplicity, and the renunciation of possessions. Each monk is expected to be engaged in labor at least five hours a day and is allowed two meals a day but is not permitted to eat meat.

As a young man studying in Rome, Benedict observed many students who were into vice. Wishing to please God alone, he abandoned his studies, left his father's home, renounced his property, and sought a solitary and holy life as a hermit living alone in a cave.

He withdrew to a remote place called Subiaco, about 50 miles from Rome.

Benedict gained a reputation for prophecy, performance of miracles, and piety. On one occasion, for example, the brothers were building a wall when it collapsed, crushing the arms and legs of a boy. Benedict had the boy brought to his tiny cell and placed on his mat while he prayed. According to legend, the boy recovered within an hour.

Benedict founded the monastery at Monte Cassino in 529 A.D., which became one of the most influential retreats in the history of Christendom. When the Lombards sacked Monte Cassino, the monks fled to Rome with a copy of Benedict's *Rule*.

Like Antony and Beatrice, Benedict embraced a number of behaviors associated with asceticism. Having renounced worldly possessions, he lived alone as a hermit in a quiet life. Further, he struggled to control his sexual temptations, and he practiced mortification.

Mental health experts have suggested that at least some famous ascetics were mentally ill. Antony's battles with the devil, for example, resemble schizophrenic hallucinations. His retreat into the wilderness, moreover, could be viewed as withdrawal, which is another symptom of schizophrenia.

MOTIVATIONAL PROFILE

How does my theory of 16 strivings for God explain asceticism? What motivates people to become monks and nuns? What is the motivational profile that would permit a person to experience asceticism as meaningful?

As summarized in Table 5-1, I am suggesting that a specific profile consisting of seven basic desires motivates asceticism. I do not expect every monk or nun to have this exact profile. Nevertheless, if we were to compute the average motivation profiles of two large groups of people—those practicing asceticism and everyone else—I believe we would find that the suggested motivational profile is strongly associated with asceticism.

Table 5-1
Motivational Profile of Asceticism

I. HIGH (STRONG) DESIRE FOR HONOR
  A. Motivates Righteousness
  B. Motivates Hyper-Vigilance to Sin
  C. Motivates Penitence
  D. Motivates Self-Discipline

II. LOW (WEAK) DESIRE FOR EATING
  A. Motivates Fasting

III. LOW (WEAK) DESIRE FOR SOCIAL CONTACT
  A. Motivates Interest in Solitude

IV. LOW (WEAK) DESIRE FOR FAMILY
  A. Motivates Interest in Solitude

V. LOW (WEAK) DESIRE FOR ROMANCE
  A. Motivates Affinity for Drabness and Plainness (no adornment)
  B. Motivates Celibacy

VI. LOW (WEAK) DESIRE FOR STATUS
  A. Motivates Humility
  B. Motivates Vows of Poverty

VII. LOW (WEAK) DESIRE FOR TRANQUILITY
  A. Motivates Mortification (self-abuse)

The pursuit of moral purity and holiness—which falls under the basic desire for honor—is the single most important motivational force driving asceticism. A high (strong) desire for honor motivates a number of ascetic behaviors such as righteousness, hyper-vigilance to sin, the practice of penitence, and self-discipline because all of these behaviors are viewed as enhancing moral character.

Honor is the basic desire that motivates moral behavior. A strong desire for honor may motivate ascetics to be much more concerned with morality than are most people. If future researchers were to ask ascetics to complete the Reiss Motivation Profile®, I predict they would score very high on the scale assessing the basic desire for honor.

Although everybody is concerned with issues of right versus wrong, ascetics differ from others in *how strongly* they desire the highest possible degree of honor. Basically they want moral purity or perfect honor. This leads to righteousness because this personality trait satisfies the desire for honor and, thus, leads to the experiences the individual wants and values. Righteous people go through everyday life judging right versus wrong. When something happens, their first thought is whether it was good (the will of God) or evil (the will of the Devil). They concentrate their energies on living a morally outstanding life.

Since ascetics seek moral purity, they avoid sin at all costs. They strive to resist temptations, impure thoughts, and sexual desire. In the language of psychology, they are hyper-vigilant to sin, setting the bar for moral behavior so high that even the most minor imperfection of character bothers them. They aim not only to resist temptations but also to avoid being tempted in the first place. Perhaps since they tend to view temptations and minor transgressions as sinful, ascetics may be quick to experience guilt.

Since ascetics seek moral purity, they may spend a significant amount of time and effort doing penitence, meditating, and praying in the hope that the divine will forgive them for their sins. The psychology of penitence is rooted in the parent-child relationship. Children learn that their parents forgive their misdeeds after punishing them. Ascetics punish themselves for their sins hoping that God, their father in heaven, will forgive them.

Ascetics view sexual desire and bodily needs as sinful. They are concerned that the needs of the body interfere with transcendental experiences and holiness. They believe the body is evil because its needs can fill their minds with thoughts of food, sex, and comfort, all of which push out conscious thoughts of God.

Ascetics value discipline and self-restraint as a means of resisting temptation and avoiding sin. They lead a disciplined life and seek to control their bodily needs to resist devilish temptations. In my motivation theory, a strong basic desire for honor motivates discipline in all its manifestations including moral discipline, military discipline, or the discipline of an athlete in training.

Fasting is a common ascetic discipline. Saints Antony, Beatrice, and Benedict all fasted frequently and for relatively long periods. John Cennick was a seventeenth century British lay preacher who also fasted long and often. He regarded dry bread as too much of an indulgence for so great a sinner as himself (James, 1918/1890, p. 265).

At first blush, one might suppose that fasting is about the basic desire for eating, but I am suggesting it is motivated by the compound motive of a high (strong) desire for honor and a low (weak) desire for eating. Fasting is undertaken not only because the individual places relatively little value on sustenance, which is motivated by a low basic desire for eating, but also because the individual seeks to be forgiven for sin, which is motivated by a high basic desire for honor. The primary goal of fasting is penitence and to be forgiven by the divine.

Jerome Kroll and Bernard Bachrach (2005) suggested that ascetics fast as a biological facilitator of mystical experiences of the divine. They cited evidence that food restriction may help some people achieve altered states of consciousness. Consistent with this possibility, Franklin (1962) described "glimpses" of the divine after days of fasting (p. 10).

A low (weak) desire for social contact motivates withdrawal from social life. Ascetics spend much of their time alone in meditation and prayer. Some move to remote or rural places, leaving behind friends and family. Saint Antony, for example, left his sister and others in his village to live alone in a cave in the wilderness. Saint Benedict left Rome for a solitary existence in a cave, although he later lived a monastic life with small groups of monks. Saint Beatrice lived apart from society in a monastery.

Ascetics embrace a quiet, solitary life because it satisfies a low desire for social contact. They seek God in private places. They embrace environments where they can meditate for sustained periods of time without being interrupted by noise or by distracting demands for small talk. As Thomas Kempis (2000) put it, "The person who wants to arrive at interiority and spirituality has to leave the crowd behind and spend some time with Jesus ... in quiet and silence the faithful soul makes progress, the hidden meanings of the Scriptures become clear, and the eyes weep with devotion every night. Even as one learns to grow still, he draws closer to the Creator and father from the hurly-burly of the world. As one divests himself of friends and acquaintances, he is visited by God and the holy angels" (p. 19).

People with a high (strong) need for social contact tend to be playful and fun loving. They like to joke around and laugh. In contrast, those with a low need for social contact tend to be serious. They dislike fooling around. As children, both Saint Antony and Saint Beatrice rarely played with their peers.

In his book chapter, "The Way of the Ascetics: Negative or Affirmative," Kallistos Ware (1995) argued that ascetics are not asocial their entire lives because in their advanced years many become spiritual advisors and teachers for younger monks and disciples. I respectfully disagree with this point of view: It is not a social event when teacher and student meet. Teaching falls under the basic desires for power (influence) and perhaps curiosity, not the basic desire for social contact, which is about interacting with peers.

Monks who live in monasteries may desire more social experiences than those who live alone. Monasteries, of course, allow for friendships to form among the brothers or among the nuns. Still the serious, non-jovial nature of monastic life suggests that many brothers and nuns have a low basic desire for social contact, although not as low as we would expect for those who embrace the solitary life in rural areas, caves, or cells.

Note how different my analysis of social motivation is from the conventional psychological view. Psychologists generally assume that social experiences are intrinsically joyful, not just for gregarious people, but potentially for everyone. So why do ascetics, loners, and introverts limit their social experiences? According to conventional psychological wisdom, it is because they lack self-confidence and are afraid of being criticized or rejected. Maybe they are ashamed of their background or social class or the neighborhood in which they live. Maybe they think they are boring or unattractive or awkward. By teaching social skills to loners and private people, and by providing gentle encouragement, psychologists aim to help shy people come out of their "shells" and socialize more often.

I reject the view that an active social life is naturally enjoyable for everyone. In contrast, I suggest that some people are born to be extroverts, and others are born to be introverts. Some are happiest with a rich social life, but others are happiest spending significant time in solitude. It depends on who we are.

Some introverts reject a rich social life not because they fear rejection, but rather because they simply don't enjoy a lot of socializing. They view socializing as a superficial experience devoid of meaning. They value the solitary life for its own intrinsic joyful qualities.

Since solitude implies the absence of both family and friends, I suggest that ascetics have a low basic desire for family in addition to a low basic desire for social contact. People who love being around children, or who embrace the role of parents, are unlikely to seek solitude.

Ascetics look for happiness and meaning outside of family life. As adults they show much less interest in children compared with the average individual. Saints Antony, Beatrice, and Benedict did not marry and had no children. Siddhartha Gautama left his family when he set out to seek a spiritual life.

We now consider why ascetics embrace drabness and plainness and renounce sex, sexual passion, and aesthetics. Monks, nuns, and Catholic priests, for example, all take vows of celibacy. Saints Antony, Beatrice, and Benedict practiced celibacy. What is it about abstinence from sex that some religious people find to be deeply meaningful?

I suggest that a low (weak) basic desire for romance is another important psychological need motivating asceticism. In this basic desire, *what* everyone wants is to manage their sexual experiences. *How much* sex is desired, however, depends on the individual. Those with a high desire for romance tend to be passionate, flirtatious, and promiscuous because these behaviors satisfy this desire.

In contrast, those with a low desire for romance tend to be Platonic, abstinent, or monogamous because these behaviors satisfy this psychological need.

According to our theory of 16 basic desires (Reiss, 2013a), low basic desires are just as important in motivating values and meaningful experiences as are high basic desires. Only average basic desires have minimal psychological significance. People with a low desire for romance, for example, are proud of not being driven or controlled by passion. They find meaning in celibacy because these experiences satisfy their needs and express their values.

A low desire for romance motivates people to devalue sex, not just to abstain from it. Both Saint Antony and Saint Benedict, for example, expressed their negative evaluation of sexual passion by attributing their carnal desires to the Devil himself. Saint Augustine suggested that sexual passion is sinful when it is independent of the biological need to reproduce. To support this view, he suggested that the "original sin" of Adam and Eve is evidence that God disapproves of sexual pleasure. Clearly, these Catholic saints held such a low opinion of sexual passion they viewed it as a significant source of sin and evil.

Ascetic celibacy may be motivated by a high (strong) desire for honor in addition to a low (weak) desire for romance. Again, a high need for honor motivates discipline and self-restraint. Ascetics may value celibacy as penitence or self-restraint, both motivated by a high need for honor.

Why do ascetics embrace a drab lifestyle? Their living quarters are Spartan and unadorned. They dress plainly. They reject color in favor of drab. A low desire for romance might motivate disinterest in color and beauty. I think human beings are interested in beauty at least partially because it arouses sexual passion. Everybody aims to appear attractive to his or her partner; nobody wants to be ugly during foreplay. People with weak sex drives are less interested in beauty than those with strong sex drives. If ascetics have weak sex drives, as I suggest, this might explain their relative lack of interest in beauty.

Personality traits come in opposites. I am suggesting that the ascetic personality type is the opposite of what might be called a romantic personality type. The romantic seeks frequent sex, but the ascetic shuns it. The romantic brags about sexual exploits, but the ascetic is ashamed of his or her sexual urges. The romantic is proud of his or her passionate nature, whereas the ascetic is proud of possessing the discipline to resist temptation. The romantic values art and beauty, but the ascetic embraces plainness.

Ascetics may choose to reside in austere, Spartan environments to assert their values. They are saying that the attractiveness of their surroundings is unimportant because it has no spiritual significance. They find meaning in rejecting all kinds of worldly pleasure, including the experience of beauty.

What motivates ascetics to embrace poverty and to renounce worldly possessions? What motivates their humility? I suggest that a low (weak) basic desire for status is part of the motivational profile for asceticism. In this basic desire, *what* everyone wants is to manage where they stand in social hierarchies. *How much* status is desired depends on the individual. People with a high need for status tend to be formal, materialistic, and proud because these behaviors are associated with high social standing. In contrast, those with a low need tend to be informal and humble because these behaviors are associated with modest social status.

People with a weak need for status reject the idea that wealth and property make an individual important. They do not believe that the social class into which we are born determines our importance. They do not put on airs to assert superiority and significance. They believe that how important we are depends on merit, not on family background, popularity, or wealth.

Ascetics express their low need for status when they embrace poverty. They believe that wealth, fame, and success are relatively insignificant. They are saying, "Wealth or high birth doesn't make a person important. Spirit does! Righteousness does!"

Attention is a primal indicator of status. People pay attention to us when they think we are important but ignore us when they think we are unimportant. Since ascetics seek a low degree of status, they try to blend into the background without attracting attention. They dress plainly so as not to stand out.

The practice of what has been called "heroic asceticism," which refers to dramatic and public displays of suffering, suggests that some monks call attention to how holy they are. Although most monks, I think, reject the need for status (social standing), these monks embrace the need for status based on holiness rather than on wealth or popularity. Unlike the average person, they do not wish to call attention to their property or success. Instead, they call attention to their piety.

Religious leaders have renounced heroic asceticism as hypocrisy. They reject seeking attention for one's piety. They have declared attention seeking to be inappropriate behavior for a monk or nun. Saint Augustine instructed ascetics to suffer in private. So does the Bible.

> *And when you fast, He says, be not as the hypocrites, sad. For they disfigure their face that they may appear unto men to fast. Amen, I say to you, they have received their reward. But you, when you fast, anoint your heads and wash your faces that you appear not to men to fast but to your Father who is in secret; and our Father who seeth in secret will repay you (Matthew 6:16-18).*

A low basic desire for status motivates people to pay little attention to their reputation. This may explain why ascetics are not intimidated when other people think they are foolish to give up their property. They are not wounded when others think they are foolish for dressing in plain clothes. They can embrace socially devalued behaviors because they are relatively unconcerned with what others think of them. The biographer of Saint Beatrice, for example, reported that even as a child Beatrice was indifferent to ridicule from peers.

To summarize, I have suggested two different reasons for why ascetics reject worldly possessions and embrace a vow of poverty.

The simple life is meaningful to them because it fulfills their desire for low status, which motivates them to value humility and to devalue attention seeking. Further, the simple life minimizes distraction from spiritual pursuits. They want to devote so much time and effort to prayer, meditation, and contemplation, they have little time for worldly pursuits.

We now consider possible psychological explanations for the ascetic practice of self-abusive mortification. Here is James's (1913/1890) description of the practices of Madeleine Sophie Barat, the founder of the Sacred Heart order:

> her love of pain and suffering was insatiable...[she said that] to live a single day without suffering for God would be intolerable...[She said she had a fever for] suffering, humiliation, and annihilation. "Nothing but pain," she continually said in her letters, "makes my life supportable" (p. 273).

James suggested that ascetic mortifications and torments might be due to pessimistic feelings about the self. He thought that ascetics have negative self-esteem because they abuse their bodies and are quick to think of themselves as sinners. I disagree with James on this point; I do not think that asceticism is associated with low self-esteem (a high need for acceptance).

People with high self-esteem are self-confident, while those with low self-esteem are insecure. Although James may be right that some ascetics have low self-esteem, others seem to have average or high self-esteem. Saint Benedict, for example, practiced self-abusive mortification but was not insecure, did not fear failure, and was not unusually sensitive to rejection. On the contrary, he confidently went about his faith healing and leading his monastery. He did not have low self-esteem.

I suggest that a low (weak) basic desire for tranquility, in combination with a high (strong) basic desire for honor, motivates many examples of self-abusive mortification. In the basic desire for tranquility, *what* everyone wants is to manage his or her experiences of anxiety and pain. *How much* anxiety and pain is desired, however, depends on the individual. Some people have a high need for tranquility, which means they cannot tolerate much anxiety and pain. Others have a low need for tranquility, which implies they are adventuresome and can tolerate much more anxiety and pain than can the average person. Those with a high desire for tranquility tend to be timid, cautious, and quick to complain about pain. In contrast, those with a low desire tend to be brave, adventurous, and slow to complain about pain. Only people with a low sensitivity for pain and anxiety could endure the self-abusive mortifications practiced by ascetics.

People who have a low desire for tranquility tend to be courageous, and some are even fearless. This may help explain how some ascetics, such as Saint Antony and Saint Benedict, live in the wilderness without being afraid of attack from wild animals or of being robbed by passing rogues.

To summarize, Table 5-1 presents the suggested motivational profile for asceticism. It implies that the personality traits associated with asceticism include righteousness, disciplined, loner, serious, humble, informal, and calm. In contrast, the personality traits associated with a rejection of asceticism are expedience, insincere, self-indulgence, gregarious, jovial, family-oriented, romantic, proud, materialistic, and timid.

REISS VS. MENNINGER

To draw a sharper distinction between my views on asceticism and those of Freudian psychiatry, I will compare my analysis with the views of psychiatrist Karl Menninger (1938), an influential figure in the mid-twentieth century when Freudian theory dominated psychiatry. According to Menninger, asceticism is motivated by an unconscious desire for self-destruction. He likened asceticism to alcoholism, which he believed expresses a wish for self-destruction.

Is self-hatred the key to understanding asceticism? Menninger and other Freudian psychiatrists have answered this question affirmatively. They say that ascetics think of themselves as sinners and therefore as unworthy of everyday pleasures and comforts. Pleasure makes them feel guilty. They reject comfort, embrace hardship, renounce property, and abuse themselves as part of their effort to manage their strong feelings of guilt.

Menninger traced the roots of asceticism to early childhood. He believed that in childhood ascetics are mistreated or abused by their parents. They assume they are unworthy of better treatment and acquire an extremely negative view of their self-worth. Such negative self-feelings are repressed in the unconscious mind but find expression in the asceticism of the adult.

Freudians assume that children who are mistreated by their parents come to believe they are unworthy of their parents' love. They struggle to control their anger out of a fear of punishment. They repress their rage into the unconscious mind where it remains latent for a while. As adults they may seem calm and gentle to people they meet casually, but beneath the surface they are still feeling anger at their parents.

Freudians also asserted that during childhood ascetics were taught that sexual desire is sinful. To avoid feeling like a sinner every time they experience sexual desire, they repress such desires into their unconscious minds. As adults they consciously think of themselves as devoted to God, but they unconsciously fear having a lustful and sinful nature. Antony's dreams of fornication with a temptress, Freudians would say, were expressions of his own unconscious sexual desires, not dirty thoughts planted by the Devil. Antony's renunciation of sensuality was an unconsciously motivated psychological defense intended to disguise his true lustful nature.

To summarize, Freudians trace the roots of adult asceticism to childhood experiences of abuse and mistreatment, which they say lead to feelings of worthlessness and guilt in addition to repression of sexual desire. How do people behave when they feel like worthless sinners? According to Freudian theory, they punish themselves in a desperate effort to alleviate their feelings of guilt, but any relief they experience from self-punishment is only temporary. No matter how much mortification they inflict on themselves, say Freudians, deep down ascetics still feel like worthless sinners.

Menninger suggested that ascetics voluntarily subject themselves to a life of hardship, starvation, sleeplessness, and flagellation because pleasure only adds to their unconscious feelings of guilt. They do not end their lives by committing suicide because they aim to prolong their suffering.

Menninger believed that ascetics abuse their bodies for the same reasons alcoholics drink themselves to death. Feeling guilty and worthless, they unconsciously wish for self-destruction to end their emotional agony. The German philosopher Friedrich Nietzsche wrote that Christianity permits only two forms of suicide—martyrdom and asceticism.

Menninger thought that the psychological function of asceticism is to disguise and ward off impulses that are consciously regarded as sinful. Ascetics become puritanical to deceive themselves into thinking they do not lust for sexual experiences. They dress plainly to deceive themselves into thinking they are disinterested in the opposite gender. These deceptions, say Freudians, help ascetics manage unconscious guilt.

Menninger presented little scientific evidence to support his view of asceticism. It may not be true, for example, that asceticism is associated with an abusive childhood. Further, there is little hard evidence that ascetics hate themselves or are particularly angry.

In contrast to Menninger's view, I suggest that religious people embrace asceticism because it is meaningful to them. They are acting in ways that express how much they value honor, solitude, humility, and tranquility. They are not expressing anger at their parents for having abused them as children.

According to Menninger, ascetics are hyper vigilant to sin because they unconsciously harbor rage toward their parents. There is no scientific method for determining whether such a statement is true or false. According to the theory of 16 strivings for God, ascetics are hyper vigilant to sin because they place a high value on honor. This hypothesis can be tested scientifically.

According to Menninger, ascetic fasting and mortification are motivated by an unconscious desire for self-destruction. According to the theory of 16 strivings, ascetic fasting and mortification are a positive assertion of the individual's values. The ascetic isn't saying symbolically, "I am a worthless sinner. I will starve myself to death because I don't deserve to live any longer." The ascetic is saying, "I value my honor above all else. I will fast to purify my soul to seek holiness."

I am suggesting that asceticism arises from normal variations in the strength of the 16 basic desires. In other words, it arises as an effort to maximize meaning when a person is born with and/or acquires the motivational profile presented in Table 5-1.

We have two psychological analyses of asceticism. On the one hand, Freudian experts studying the unconscious mind say that asceticism is motivated by guilt and rage. On the other hand, I study the conscious mind and suggest that asceticism is motivated by the basic desires delineated in Table 5-1.

Our discussion of asceticism would be incomplete without consideration of its resemblance to the symptoms of two mental illnesses, anorexia and schizophrenia. In anorexia nervosa people starve themselves, possibly to death if medical intervention isn't initiated. Although this sometimes resembles ascetic fasting, there are important differences. Ascetics fast as part of a deliberately chosen religious lifestyle, whereas people with anorexia nervosa starve themselves in reaction to loss or anxiety. The ascetic aims to please God, but in anorexia the patient is committing suicide.

Schizophrenia, a mental illness which is caused at least partially by biochemical disturbances of the brain, can produce behaviors similar to asceticism. Standing motionless for long periods of time, embracing filth, and pillar sitting, for example, are symptoms of schizophrenia. Kroll and Bachrach (2005, p. 25) among others have presented case examples of people who seem to be practicing asceticism but actually have schizophrenia. One young man diagnosed with schizophrenia, for example, had a habit of standing motionless for over thirty hours while praying in his apartment. His behavior improved significantly when he was given anti-psychotic medication. In this case the prayer and odd posture were likely caused by mental illness, not the profile of basic desires shown in Table 5-1. Although mental illness may play a role in asceticism practiced by some individuals, our theory implies that many individuals who practice asceticism are mentally healthy.

6

WHAT MOTIVATES MYSTICISM?

We now examine how the 16 basic desires might play out in mystical experiences. These are usually short-term, discrete, well-defined trances that can be recalled from memory. In these states the individual senses the presence of the divine. As one person described it, "I have experienced God's presence... I have been lifted out of myself in a state of pure ecstatic joy" (Pratt, 1921, p. 356).

William James (2004/1902) believed that religion is rooted in mystical experiences. Consistent with this view, psychologist David Fontana (2003) noted that every influential religion originated as a consequence of a mystical experience by its founder. He wrote, "Moses talked with Jehovah, Christ heard the voice of God at his baptism, Mohammed was visited by the Angel Gabriel..." (p. 21).

Buddhism was inspired by the mystical experience of Siddhartha Gautama. He became the Buddha, or "one who is awake", when he had an experience of a single, unmoving, unchanging, serene reality. He envisioned an endless cycle of birth and rebirth for all people and things. The only escape from this "wheel of karma" was to become conscious of the unity of all reality. This state of enlightenment leads to an experience called *nirvana*, in which pain and suffering no longer exist.

People who have had mystical experiences generally describe them similarly regardless of culture. The features of mystical experiences include feelings of unity, sacredness, passivity, ineffability, and joy. Questionnaire-based research has confirmed these self-reports (Hood, Hill, & Spilka, 2009). Approximately one-third to one-half of Americans surveyed endorsed having had a mystical experience or religious awakening (Hood, Hill, & Spilka, 2009). Walter Stace (1960) and Ralph Wilbur Hood (1975) pioneered modern scholarship on mystical experiences.

ALTERED STATES OF CONSCIOUSNESS

Some psychiatrists regard mysticism as an "Altered State of Consciousness" (ASC), or experience in which the individual may perceive and think in unusual ways. ASCs include hypnotic trances and coma. Drugs or high fever can induce ASCs; dancing, chanting, and certain breathing exercises can facilitate them.

In 1995 I had an ASC experience when I was hospitalized with an infection in my liver ducts (cholangitis). As I watched a televised football game from my bed, my temperature started to rise quickly to more than 105°F. For 20 minutes or so I had the most vivid perceptions of my life—experiencing incredibly beautiful colors and sounds and visiting with my deceased parents who were very happy to see me and I them. When my fever started to break, I didn't want to return to reality. I wanted to stay in my altered state with its beautiful colors, sounds, and memories. For the first time in my life I no longer wanted to live because death—or what I assumed was death—seemed so much more pleasant. It was an overwhelming, intensely pleasurable reality unlike any I had previously known. I experienced it as more "real" than I typically experienced the sensory world. Since then I have had two similar ASCs, both when I was very ill and near death. (As a liver transplant patient, I have come close to dying on multiple occasions.)

Some scientists have suggested that the use of psychedelic drugs by prehistoric humans might have induced ASCs/mystical experiences that led to the emergence of religion. In 1953 Aldous Huxley experimented with mescaline in the hope of gaining extraordinary insights. He published his experiences in his book *The Doors of Perception.* He wrote that mescaline intensifies sensory experiences and observed that it has been used for thousands of years in the religious ceremonies of Native American tribes.

Psilocybin is a hallucinogen produced by more than 200 different species of mushrooms. It induces euphoria, altered perceptions of time, and visual and mental hallucinations. Various tribes use it in their religious ceremonies (Guzmán, 2008; Metzner, 2004). After ingesting psilocybin while vacationing in Mexico, former Harvard University psychologist Timothy Leary sought to study drug-induced ASCs. Many of the participants in Leary's studies reported mystical and spiritual experiences while under the influence of psilocybin.

Huston Smith, an influential religious scholar who first used psilocybin while visiting Leary, described his ASC experience as authentic. "I had no doubt that my experience was valid," he wrote. He believed he had become conscious of transcendental reality, "because it was retracing exactly what I was convinced was the nature of reality" (Smith, 1991, p. 27).

In a 1957 *Life* magazine article, American scientist R. Gordon Wasson described his experiences ingesting psilocybin-containing mushrooms during a traditional religious ceremony of the Mazatec Indians of Mexico. In 1986 Wasson suggested that psilocybin might have played a significant role in the origin of religion. Imagery found on prehistoric murals and rock paintings in modern-day Spain and Algeria indicate that ancient human artists had consumed mushrooms that contained psilocybin. Wasson suggested possible connections between the ingestion of these mushrooms, the emergence of language in human evolution, and the emergence of consciousness.

We now know that psychedelic drugs can induce religious experiences, which are subjectively indistinguishable from spontaneously-occurring mystical experiences. Nevertheless, the use of psychedelic drugs as a spirituality-enhancing agent is controversial. Many religious authorities oppose the use of psychedelics for this purpose.

The idea that intoxication has spiritual significance and expands consciousness was expressed in the mythology of ancient Greece. Dionysus, or Bacchus in Roman mythology, is the god of wine, mystical excitement, and male sexuality. He inspired festivals with wild dancing in the street, ecstatic behavior, and epic sessions of drunken merrymaking.

Today, many religious ceremonies make use of intoxicating drugs. The Jewish Passover Seder requires men to drink four cups of wine. Cannabis (called bhang) has long been part of Hindu practice among sadhu and siddhi, but it is not part of the general Hindu tradition. Islam, however, forbids the use of intoxicants.

ASCs can be induced by various ascetic practices, which are the same the world over. These methods "transform the thinking man into a hypnotic subject and substitute emotion for volition and sentiment for morality" (Pratt, 1921, p. 373). Ascetic practices include dancing, reciting hymns, chanting, drumming, and reading poems. The experience of beauty—such as the majesty of a mountain or the appreciation of art—can trigger mystical experience. In *The Seven Storey Mountain*, Thomas Merton, a monk and modern mystic, wrote extensively about the influence that art had on his childhood spiritual development.

In some eastern religions, the practice of yoga refers to physical and mental exercises that prepare the body for deep meditation, leading to mystical experience or Samadhi. Yoga, which means "yoke," refers to the union between the human spirit and the divine. The yogi learn how to control breath and body to isolate consciousness from sights and sounds. These practices may increase ASCs.

DIVIDED SELF

Freud applied his theory of psychic structures and human development to explain mystical experiences. In Freud's theory the id is the source of instinctual urges for sex and aggression. It is present at birth and operates in accordance with a "primary process" of wish-fulfilling fantasy, dreams, and daydreams. In the primary process the individual does not recognize the difference between fantasy and reality. An example is a hungry boy trying to eat a toy because he imagines the toy is food.

The ego emerges shortly after birth to manage the desires of the id and to satisfy survival needs. The ego functions in accordance with a secondary process of rational thinking; it recognizes the difference between fantasy and reality. The secondary process guides the hungry child to eat food rather than some inappropriate object such as a plastic toy. In the normal course of human development, the secondary process of the ego supersedes the primary process of the id because reality-based thinking is more effective in satisfying our needs than is fantasy-based thought.

Freud spoke of "psychic boundaries" separating the reality-focused ego from the fantasy-based id. He viewed mysticism as resulting from a breakdown in the boundary between the ego and id; he thought that mystics temporarily regress to the primary process and, as a consequence, confuse fantasy for reality. Romain Rolland, a personal friend of Freud, used the metaphor "oceanic feelings" to refer to how this regression to the primary process is experienced. Although Rolland suggested that oceanic feelings have spiritual significance, Freud disagreed. Freud rejected the idea that fantasy-based thinking is a valid source of religion.

Freudians analyzed mystic visions as hallucinations (seeing things that aren't there), similar to what occurs in the mental illness schizophrenia; they did not consider mystic visions to result from contact with transcendent reality. Freudians interpreted mystical dialogue with the divine or devil as auditory hallucination (hearing voices or sounds that do not exist), which is another symptom of schizophrenia. They suggested that the mystic's desire for union with God corresponds to the infant's wish for union with the mother, and that the mystic's desire for oneness with all creation expresses a regression to the narcissistic grandiosity of an early infantile state. Both of these infantile wishes may be symptoms of schizophrenia. Further, psychoanalyst Franz Alexander (2001/1932) suggested that mystical rapture is very much like the catatonic ecstasy of people with schizophrenia.

Various researchers attempted to determine if the Freudian hypothesis of a correspondence between schizophrenia and mysticism is valid. Contrary to Freud's ideas, the results of these studies showed no such correspondence. Pratt (1921), for example, published a study showing significant differences between mystical and schizophrenic experiences. Unlike schizophrenics, mystics tend to possess an outstanding strength of will dedicated to the pursuit of the divine. More recent researchers have shown that mysticism is associated with positive psychological states of being, while mental illnesses such as schizophrenia are associated with negative psychological states.

Carl Jung (1923, 1933, 1960) offered a different view of how unconscious fantasy-based thinking plays out in mystical experiences. Whereas Freud saw the unconscious mind as a cesspool of our darkest desires, Jung viewed intuition and fantasy as possible sources of creative energy, meaningful experiences, and enlightenment. Jung advanced a favorable view of mysticism and the eastern religions that practice it.

In some of the most interesting psychological ideas ever published, Jung (1911/1977, 1923) analyzed the nature of human consciousness. He asked: What is thinking? What is its essential nature? How do images, visions, words, feelings, and instincts play out in human thought? He distinguished between two types of thinking: directed thinking (thinking in words) and fantasy-based thinking (thinking in images). In directed thinking—examples include logical thinking, scientific analysis, and all rational thinking—we aim to conform our thoughts to reality or truth. In fantasy thinking—examples include intuition, dreams, daydreams, and visions—we express our wishes. Jung believed that fantasy-based thinking wells up from an inner, instinctual source deeply rooted in human nature.

Jung viewed the human psyche as divided between a conscious part, which thinks in words, and an unconscious part, which thinks in images. Jung (1960) asserted that we live in a state of lost unity and harmony between our conscious and unconscious experiences—and that mysticism is an attempt to unify the self at a higher level of consciousness. According to Jung, the recovery of this lost unity is the primary concern of both religion and psychology.

Jung's analysis of directed versus fantasy-based thinking was similar to Freud's distinction between primary and secondary processes. Jung's "divided self" is similar to Freud's division of the self into ego versus id. (Freud also suggested a third part of the psyche, called the superego, but it is not relevant here.)

Both Jung and Freud embraced the idea of primary process, fantasy-based thinking. They differed, however, on the origin of the primary process. Freud traced primary process thinking to the individual's infantile and early childhood experiences. In contrast, Jung traced fantasy-based thinking to the dawn of our species, before the development of language, when humans communicated in pictures rather than words. Whereas Freud thought that myths and dreams carry us back to our early childhood, Jung believed that myths and dreams carry us back to the origins of human culture.

Abraham Maslow (1994) suggested that religion is rooted in mystical experiences, which he called "peak experiences." He did not believe that peak experiences are true encounters with the divine; he thought of them as the result of human growth, which he called the self-actualizing tendency. He disputed the Freudian view that mysticism is related to mental illnesses such as schizophrenia.

Maslow predicted that "self-actualized" people—loosely defined as people who are mature, healthy, productive, and genuine—are more likely to have "peak experiences." He tested this prediction by asking 270 people to provide written descriptions of ecstatic moments in their life. He defined these as transitory experiences of bliss, ecstasy, joy, awe, reverence, and wonder.

Maslow discovered that peak experiences are quite common and have been reported by diverse individuals from many walks in life. As Borchert (1994) observed, "mystics include both the stolid and the emotional types, both the balanced and the unstable, the physically strong and the frail" (p. 47). A tendency to have mystical experiences is not a sign of superior human development. This does not mean, however, that a person's basic desires and values are unrelated to how often the person has mystical experiences.

MOTIVATIONAL PROFILE OF A MYSTIC

We have considered four very different views on the psychological origin of mysticism.

1) Some neuropsychologists suggested that mysticism is an ASC induced by drugs, high fever, and perhaps other biological events. They have speculated on the possibility that religion began when primitive societies discovered certain hallucinogenic drugs.

2) Freudians suggested that mysticism is the result of psychic processes similar to what happens in schizophrenia when the individual confuses fantasy for reality.

3) Jungians asserted that mysticism may be an effort to expand consciousness to include certain primal experiences that are retained in the unconscious mind.

4) Maslow thought that mysticism is a consequence of human development or what he called becoming the best we can be.

Here we consider a fifth, new possibility in which mysticism is an attempt to satisfy five basic desires. This theory implies that mysticism is a normal expression of certain values deeply held by some people but not by others. It is unrelated to mental illness.

Table 6-1 presents five core values expressed in mystical experiences in their approximate order of significance as well as the basic desires that motivate them. The list is based on what mystics themselves have said about such experiences. Table 6-1 identifies harmony and unity as the two most important core values expressed in mysticism because many mystics have typically spoken very positively about the harmonious nature of their visions and the psychological sense of unity/interconnectedness they experience.

Table 6-1

Five Core Values Expressed in Mystical Experiences

CORE VALUE	BASIC DESIRE
Harmony	Low Vengeance
Unity	Low Independence
Awareness	Low Curiosity
Passivity	Low Power
Beauty	Average Romance

The mystic vision is one of absolute harmony. It is character-ized by stillness, calm, quietude, and serenity. In such harmonious states there is no strife, agitation, anger, competition, confrontation, or struggle. Some reports of mystical visions describe encounters with the Devil, which certainly implies strife, but the vast majority of reports of mystical experiences affirm the quality of harmony.

Since a very low/very weak desire for vengeance motivates people to value harmony, I suggest that people with a weak desire for vengeance are significantly more likely to have mystical trances than are those with an average or high desire for vengeance. According to the theory of 16 basic desires, people with a low need for vengeance go through everyday life seeking to experience minimal or no strife. They avoid confrontations. Some may have a Peacemaker personality type. In contrast, people with a high desire for vengeance go through everyday life embracing confrontation at almost every opportunity. Some may have a Warrior personality type. What my theory implies is that people who have a Peacemaker personality type may have more mystical experiences than those who have a Warrior personality type because Peacemakers should be much more likely than Warriors to seek out and value mystical harmony. Further, Peacemakers should experi-ence mystical states of consciousness as highly meaningful, perhaps as glimpses of transcendent reality, whereas Warriors should expe-rience these states as frustrating because they are devoid of the strife the individual seeks.

At first blush, we might suppose that the basic desire for tranquility motivates people to value harmony. According my theory of 16 basic desires, however, a high desire for tranquility motivates people to seek safety, not harmony. I think safety and security are different from harmony. I think harmony is about peacefulness, or the absence of strife itself. I predict that a low (weak) basic desire for vengeance, not a high (strong) basic desire for tranquility, is a significant motivator of mystical harmony.

Although a low desire for vengeance is predicted to increase significantly the frequency of mystical trances, other basic desires are predicted to play a role, too. A weak desire for independence—that is, a strong desire for *inter*dependence—is predicted to motivate the mystical vision of unity and interconnectedness of all reality because this vision satisfies the desire. In the theory of 16 basic desires, people with an Interdependent personality type value knowing they can count on others to meet their needs. I suspect that interdependence (low/weak desire for independence) motivates the sense of "oneness" evident in mysticism. In many reports of mystical experience the individual perceives a unity or interconnectedness to all reality, so much so that some say the sense of an ego, or "I-ness," is temporarily lost. Some mystics report experiencing a union of ego with the Absolute, or a loosening of boundaries so that everything is perceived in consciousness as being part of the larger Universe. I think such perceptions are likely to be valued by Interdependent people, who tend to seek connections with others. By contrast, people with a high desire for independence tend to be proud, individualistic, and perhaps even stubborn. They may feel uncomfortable with perceptions of interconnectedness because they value their freedom.

In addition to low desires for vengeance and independence, mysticism may be motivated by a low (weak) need for curiosity. This doesn't mean that mystics are unintelligent or poorly educated; it means that they may value intuition and enlightenment more than they value logic and scientific knowledge. There is plenty of evidence to support this view. Mystics say that religion is about emotion, feelings, and intuition, and not about logic, rationality, or philosophy. Numerous mystics have suggested that intellectual pursuits such as science and logic are inadequate for learning about transcendent reality. Knowledge of the Absolute, for them, is revealed intuitively in visions, insights, perceptions, and expansion of consciousness. Mystics claim that the understanding gained through experience is deeper and more fundamental than the understanding gained through scientific knowledge. Whereas students of science learn facts, mystics claim enlightenment, which is an understanding of what those facts actually mean. All this suggests that in terms of the 16 basic desires, mystics express values associated with a low (weak) need for curiosity.

Here are some additional indications that low curiosity may contribute to the motivation of mystical trances. Many mystics have little interest in dogma or theology. Religion for them is a personal experience, not an intellectual or social activity. Carl Jung (1960) suggested that institutional religion, such as Judaism and Christianity, actually gets in the way of true mystical visions. As Pratt (1921) described it, "In mystical states of consciousness, insights and revelations occur suddenly, not as conclusions of rational analysis, but rather as an enlightenment knowledge...." (Pratt, 1921, p. 337). Mystical experiences are sometimes said to be "ineffable," meaning that the intellect cannot comprehend them. Much like poets who struggle to capture the meaning of love and beauty, mystics struggle to describe their experiences of the Absolute. Both poets and mystics say they never fully capture in words the essence of beauty, love, or truth. Thus the mystic uses suggestive terms such as "the Beyond," "the Absolute," "Oneness," "Reality," "Being," or simply "God."

A low need for curiosity might explain the non-intellectual values sometimes expressed by mystics. Mysticism is usually described as an emotional experience that isn't rational or intellectual. As James (1918/1890) observed, we can become acquainted with God, but we cannot explain to others what we have learned. We thus urge them to embrace mystical experiences themselves. The ancient Roman philosopher Plotinus recognized the ineffability of mystical experience. "We have no knowledge or concept of it, and we do not say it, but we say something about it" (Pratt, 1921, p. 337).

Thus far we have considered which of the 16 basic desires might motivate the qualities of harmony and unity associated with mystical experiences as well as what might motivate the mystic's perception of enlightenment. We now consider the quality of passivity—one of the four significant qualities of mystical experience identified by William James in his influential study of the varieties of mystical experience. Passivity refers to a surrender of will to the life movement of the universe. The mystic, we are told, has no desire to change or improve anything, but instead passively accepts reality as is.

According to my theory of 16 basic desires, a low/weak basic desire for power may motivate the mystic's passivity or surrender of will to the Absolute. Since people who have a low need for power dislike trying to control events, they tend to be passive. Some may value letting go of their emotions because flow satisfies their low (weak) desire for power. In contrast, people with a high (strong) desire for power tend to be assertive, not passive. Since they may value controlling their emotions and resist letting go, they may devalue the passivity associated with mystical trances.

We now consider how the basic desire for romance might play out in mystical experiences. This basic desire motivates people both to value beauty and to seek sex. Although mystics value beauty, it is doubtful if they have an above-average sex drive. Their desire for romance does not seem to be strong enough to motivate a strong sex drive, nor is it weak enough to motivate them to embrace drabness. By definition, average basic desires are neither strong nor weak.

There are a number of considerations consistent with the view that the perception of beauty typically is an important quality in mystical experience. Mystical experiences are often described as too beautiful for words. The perception of beautiful scenery, such as the beauty of mountains and oceans, is a common trigger for mystical experience. Hegel, a nineteenth century German philosopher, once commented that beauty is the spiritual making itself known sensuously.

Although mystical experiences sometime have qualities sugges-tive of sexual union, I doubt if sexual motivation plays much of a role in mysticism. Pratt (1921) observed that mystics have a "love of the romantic" (p. 363). Borchart (1994) suggested that mystical experiences are like love itself. The rapture and ecstasy of an intense mystical experience may resemble sexual experience. Yet I doubt if mysticism is about sex because people with a strong sex drive tend to have many partners and devote much of their time to romance, not to the pursuit of spirituality.

In summary my theory of 16 basic desires offers an original analysis of mysticism. It implies that mysticism is typically moti-vated by five basic desires acting in combination. This view is quite different from the Freudian idea that mysticism is a regression to an infantile state of primary process thinking similar to schizo-phrenia. It is very different from the Jungian view that mystics are motivated by the perception of a divided self and a desire to recon-nect with unconscious experiences. It disputes Maslow's view that human growth prepares people for peak experiences. On the contrary, the theory of 16 basic desires implies that mysticism is a positive affirmation of five values. These values have nothing to do with infantile stages of thinking. They are conscious, not uncon-scious. They are normal values unrelated to mental illness. They have nothing to do with self-actualization or human growth, but they are strongly related to individuality and personality types.

MYSTIC PERSONALITY TYPE

As summarized in Table 6-2, the theory of 16 basic desires suggests that people with certain personalities, desires, and values may be much more likely than are others to have mystical encoun-ters. I am not suggesting, of course, that every mystic has these desires, values, and traits, only that there are significant associations and correlations. I am suggesting that the basic desires listed in Table 6-2 may be statistically associated with how many mystical encounters a person experiences.

How might the suggested motivational profile lead to actual mystical experiences? How does it happen, for example, that people who highly value harmony have mystical experiences in which harmony is actually experienced? What is the psychological basis for supposing that people who place high value on interconnectedness will actually experience such unity? Why would someone who places a high value on aesthetics experience incredibly beautiful sights and sounds?

By their effects on people's expectations and beliefs, the basic desires motivating mystical experiences could actually precipitate such experiences. The person who has a Mystic personality type seeks subjective experiences of harmony, unity, insight, solitude, passivity, and beauty. Psychologists have learned that expectations of subjective experiences sometimes produce the very experiences people expect.

In his scholarly book, *Changing Expectations,* Irving Kirsch (1990) discussed his concept of "response expectancy." He argues that the power of suggestion is so strong it can cause people to experience what they expect to experience. If a hypnotist suggests a particular subjective experience, for example, the subject might actually have that experience. Similarly, in placebo drugs the expectation of improvement in the symptoms of an illness produce the very improvements people expect.

Many people view mystics as spiritual people who for one reason or another feel the call of the divine deep within their souls. They devote themselves to the pursuit of holiness. Some join monasteries, while others practice mysticism on their own. They embrace various disciplines for expanding consciousness, like meditation, prayer, or ascetic practices. Some may use alcohol or other drugs to facilitate spiritual experiences.

This view suggests that anybody can become a mystic depending on whether or not the person is called. It is not about who you are, but whether or not you are called. If you experience an altered state of consciousness for whatever reason, the experience might transform you.

In contrast, the theory of 16 strivings for God suggests that some people are much more likely to value and find meaning in mystical experiences than are others. Table 6-2 shows five traits that, in theory, comprise a "Mystic Personality Type."

Table 6-2

The Mystic Personality Type
Gentle
Humble
Visionary
Unambitious
Aesthetic

7

RELIGION AND THE CONTRADICTIONS OF HUMAN NATURE

In order to appeal to many different kinds of people, a religion must express the values associated with a comprehensive range of basic desires, not just one or two of them. I would not go so far as to suggest that every popular religion must address all 16 basic desires, but I think a religion cannot be popular unless it addresses at least 12-13 of them. A religion that addressed only a few basic desires would be focused on such a narrow aspect of human experience its appeal could be to only part of the population.

In this chapter we will consider evidence documenting how the 16 basic desires play out in religion. We will review each of the 16 basic desires, one at a time, and then we will consider the religious beliefs and practices that seem to express that desire. We will learn that the Judeo-Christian religions express all 16 basic desires, not just one or two of them.

The 16 basic desires make us individuals. We are individuals to a much greater degree than is recognized in most previous theories of religion. Everybody embraces the 16 basic desires, but individuals prioritize them differently. How an individual prioritizes the 16 basic desires is called a Reiss Motivation Profile®. Extroverts, for example, place above-average valuation on social contact; they are gregarious because they seek many social experiences. Introverts place below-average valuation on social contact; they are quiet because they seek few social experiences. The two personality types hold opposite values. Extroverts value fun and fellowship, while Introverts value serious demeanor and solitude.

In order to have mass appeal a religion must meet two psychological criteria. It must express all, or nearly all, of the 16 basic desires, and it must express both high and low valuations of each basic desire. If a religion teaches that God blesses fellowship, it expresses the values of Extroverts. If a religion teaches that God blesses solitude, it expresses the values of Introverts. A religion cannot have mass appeal if it supports the values of those with one personality trait but not those with the opposite trait and opposite values. In order to appeal to the masses, a religion must express the values of both Extroverts and Introverts and all who combine extroversion and introversion in various proportions.

Religion can accommodate diverse spiritual personalities by providing the faithful with two kinds of experiences: those that express values associated with strong versions of the basic desires, and those that express values associated with weak versions of the same basic desires. To understand the underlying logic, imagine a world in which everyone sought to drink water at a different temperature, from cold to hot. Instead of providing people with a million different water temperatures to match their needs, we could provide them with two pitchers, one filled with very cold water and the other filled with very hot water, and let them combine water from the pitchers in any proportion necessary to produce a desired water temperature. Analogously, institutional religion can address the full range of human needs by providing the faithful with some phenomena that express strong basic desires, and with other phenomena that express weak basic desires, so that individuals can pick and choose and combine them to meet their needs.

In this chapter we will learn that the Judeo-Christian religions express each of the 16 basic desires, and that they express both strong and weak versions of each desire. In total the chapter is intended to offer significant initial support for our thesis of 16 strivings for God.

THE STRIVING FOR SALVATION

Since acceptance makes us feel good about ourselves while rejection makes us feel bad, you might think everybody always aims to feel accepted, but this is not the case. People actually regulate how much acceptance and praise they can comfortably experience. At least this was the conclusion of psychologists who studied the research topic called "self-reward" during the 1960s and 1970s (Kanfer & Phillips, 1970). In these studies children or college students performed some task in a psychological laboratory and then decided how much reward to give themselves for their performance. Surprisingly few people gave themselves the maximum reward; most chose a moderate amount of reward consistent with how well they thought they did on the experimental task.

Mental health professionals have reported case examples of people who reject praise when they feel they don't deserve it. Joey, for example, was a third-grade student I once worked with who had such a poor opinion of himself he tore up one of his drawings while his teacher was making a fuss over it. We are all a little like Joey was, rejecting praise when we think it is undeserved, but few of us would go so far as to destroy something we made just because it drew favorable comment from others.

Most people seek praise only to the extent they feel they deserve it. They feel uncomfortable when given what they think is undeserved praise. Some people squirm when told how good-looking they are because they think they are plain-looking. Others feel uncomfortable when being told what a great meal they cooked because they doubt their skills and do not wish to raise expectations for the future.

Self-confident and Insecure people vary considerably in how strongly they need to feel accepted by others. Self-confident people have a positive self-concept and need relatively little acceptance from others. An occasional pat on the back suits them just fine. They tend to have an optimistic, can-do outlook on life. Although they may feel anxious when others evaluate them at work, school, or elsewhere—most everybody does—they have the potential to learn from constructive feedback.

On the other hand, Insecure people tend to be self-critical and typically look to others to build them up. They strongly desire acceptance from others. Some need frequent reassurance and are easily devastated at the slightest criticisms. Many Insecure people have a pessimistic outlook on life, especially in regard to how things will work out for them. They may be moody and inconsistent, and they may tend to react anxiously to being evaluated by others. They may not listen when others yell at or criticize them.

Most people have an average need for acceptance, which means they are self-confident sometimes and insecure other times. One person, for example, might be self-confident about his or her ability to adjust to changing circumstances, but insecure about his or her organizational skills. Someone else might be self-confident about doing well in school but not in social situations.

For a religion to address the needs of both Self-confident and Insecure people, and those of everybody in between, it needs to provide two kinds of experiences: those that increase feelings of acceptance and, thus, make people feel self-confident, and those that decrease feelings of acceptance and, thus, make people feel insecure. As shown in Table 7-1, some religious beliefs and practices increase feelings of acceptance and self-confidence, while other beliefs and practices decrease such feelings. Individuals pick and choose the mix that is most meaningful for them.

I contend that the basic desire for acceptance motivates interest in salvation and damnation. Salvation is the greatest acceptance human beings can imagine, while its opposite, damnation, is the greatest imaginable rejection. Salvation implies that God accepts us, and it encourages people to accept themselves. They think, "I

Table 7-1

Religion and Feelings of Acceptance	
INCREASES FEELING ACCEPTED	**DECREASES FEELING ACCEPTED**
Salvation/Heaven	Damnation/Hell
Goodness of Human Nature	Original Sin/Sin
Forgiveness, Confession	Day of Judgment
Positive Thinking	Negative Thinking

must be worthy to be accepted by God." Even when others reject them, such as when they lose a romantic interest or job, their faith in divine salvation rebuilds their psychological sense of being accepted and, thus, their self-confidence.

On the other hand, thoughts about the possibility of being damned or forsaken by God reduce the sense of acceptance and, thus, make people feel bad about themselves. Deep down, people assume they must be unworthy or even worthless to be damned by God. This leads to feelings of self-dislike, insecurity, and a lack of self-confidence.

The psychology here is similar to how young children react when they are accepted or rejected by a parent. When parents have an accepting attitude, the child feels worthy and self-confident. When parents have a rejecting attitude, the child feels unworthy and insecure. The child wonders what is wrong with him or her for the parents to reject, abandon, or criticize.

The human need to manage feelings of acceptance and self-confidence motivates religious dogma about the goodness versus wickedness of human nature. Muslims, for example, believe that human nature is good. This belief supports the value of acceptance and encourages self-confidence. Because people are basically good, Islam teaches the faithful to respect other people.

On the other hand, the Roman Catholic belief in original sin implies that we are born wicked and in a fallen state from God. The more a person reflects on the meaning of original sin, the greater is the potential for negative self-feelings. Sin separates us from God and, thus, decreases satisfaction of the basic desire for acceptance. When the faithful sin, or when they just think about their sins, they may imagine God disapproving of their conduct.

Norman Vincent Peale (1952) taught that faith in God leads to self-confidence, which in turn leads to success. He encouraged the faithful to think positively and optimistically. In contrast, negative thinkers dwell on their sins and shortcomings and expect to fail. They may expect to be damned or rejected by God. Negative thinking can be self-fulfilling because people who anticipate failure and rejection do not give good efforts.

In summary, people vary in how much acceptance they desire. Self-confident people seek relatively low degrees of acceptance; Insecure people seek relatively high degrees; and everybody else falls between these two groups. To help the faithful manage their experiences of acceptance to the psychological level most meaningful to them, religion offers beliefs and practices that increase perceptions of acceptance and, thus, validate self-liking, as well as beliefs and practices that decrease perceptions of acceptance and, thus, reduce feelings of confidence. When a person of faith feels rejected, the individual can increase feelings of acceptance by anticipation of salvation or positive thinking. When a person of faith feels overconfident or undeservedly praised, the individual can decrease feelings of acceptance by reflecting on his or her sins and wickedness.

THE STRIVING FOR UNDERSTANDING

The basic desire for curiosity motivates people to seek intellectual, rational, or scientific understanding. Thinkers, who have a strong desire, embrace intellectual pursuits. They may be contemplative, inquisitive, reflective, and thoughtful because these traits satisfy their high need for intellectual curiosity.

I am an example of a Thinker. I spent 57 uninterrupted years in school as a student or college professor before finally retiring to write books and teach my theory of motivation. Over the course of my life, I have spent many thousands of days absorbed in intellec-

Table 7-2
Religion and Intellectual Curiosity

ENCOURAGES DEEP THINKING	DISCOURAGES DEEP THINKING
Divine Omniscience	Divine Enlightenment
Logos	Fundamentalism
Theology	Heresy
Logical Proofs	Revelation, Faith
Scientific Encouragement	Doctrine of Infallibility

tual pursuits. That is a lot of thinking! And I know professors who have spent more time thinking about things than I have.

In contrast, Doers, who have a weak basic desire, embrace practical pursuits. Some Doers may dislike thinking for longer than a few minutes at a time and, thus, have little patience with intellectual matters. Some are action-oriented and practical. Table 7-2 shows some of the religious beliefs and practices that address the basic desire for curiosity.

The conception of God as omniscient, and the belief that truth has a divine origin, validate the values of Thinkers and enhance satisfaction of the human desire for understanding and wisdom. The Koran expresses God's omniscience thusly: "He knows what is in the land and in the sea; no leaf falls but he knows it; nor is there a grain in the darkness under the earth, nor a thing, green or sere, but it is recorded" (6:12-59). Further, Aristotle's (1953/330 BCE) god of pure reason is an expression of the values of Thinkers.

In contrast, the Buddhist concept of enlightenment is about intuition and insight. It expresses the values of people with a weak basic desire for intellectual curiosity. According to Jung (1923, 1960) consciousness is about images and perceptions, not logic and words.

Theologians partially satisfy their intellectual needs by pondering the "logos", or divine reason. They expand dogma and assist in the propagation of a religious tradition. They write original treatises on various topics such as logical efforts to prove the existence of God, the concepts of immortality and afterlife, and why God allows evil and wickedness rather than just wiping them out.

Psychologically, the religious concept of revelation decreases intellectual curiosity and, thus, expresses the values of Doers. God reveals himself, and in so doing, he bypasses the intellect. The idea of divine revelation, if you will, puts religious intellectuals in their place. It is fine to be a Thinker, but you do not need to think to know God. When it comes to the greatest knowledge and wisdom in the universe, that which comes from knowing God, some religions teach that the intellect is not essential.

In fundamentalism Holy Scripture is taken as literal, historical truth. Fundamentalism discourages intellectual curiosity. It suggests there is little need to worry about the logical inconsistency of religious dogma or the historical inconsistencies of the Bible, as they were carefully documented by Bart D. Ehrman (2010) in *Jesus, Interrupted: Revealing the Hidden Contradictions in the Bible.*

Heresy is another religious concept that discourages deep thinking. When Galileo turned his telescope to the heavens, for example, he discovered that the sun was the center of the solar system. Since this contradicted the Church's view that the Earth is the center of the solar system, Galileo was put under house arrest and forced to repent by punitive actions that were clearly intended to intimidate free thinkers and discourage deep thinking.

St. Thomas Aquinas (1961/1259) put forth five logical proofs, which the Catholic Church still accepts as valid, for the existence of God. Logical proofs suggest that reason is so important God has chosen it as a method of revealing himself. The Thinkers in the church hierarchy wanted God to be proved logically because this would validate their intellectual values, but the Doers rejected logical proofs. Some philosophers teach that God must be accepted or rejected based on faith because he cannot be proved based on scientific observation or logical syllogism.

The modern Catholic Church encourages scientific inquiry, but under the doctrines of infallibility and revelation, it also claims to know many answers in advance of research. By claiming to already know the answers to key scientific issues, the Church discourages the very scientific inquiry it claims it wants to encourage. The Church seems to be saying to intellectuals, "Go ahead and think all you want. Since we already know the answers, though, there is no need to take your activity too seriously. If you arrive at a conclusion that contradicts Church doctrine, your work is just preliminary. When you continue with it in greater depth, eventually you will see that the Church's position is valid."

Islam is tolerant of scientific inquiry. It imbues scientific inquiry with divine significance by teaching that nature is one with God and, thus, worthy of study. From the eighth to sixteenth centuries, Islamic science was far advanced compared to its European counterpart.

In summary, the basic desire of curiosity motivates people to engage in intellectual activity, but individuals vary in how much intellectual activity they typically desire. Thinkers seek a relatively high degree of intellectual activity, Doers aim for a relatively low degree, and everybody else falls between these two types. Religion addresses the needs of both Thinkers and Doers and everybody in between them. To help the faithful manage their intellectual life to the intensity and level most meaningful to them, religion offers a number of beliefs and practices that increase intellectual activity and/or express the values of Thinkers; it also offers other beliefs and practices that decrease intellectual activity and/or express the values of Doers. Each person of faith can use these religious phenomena to help manage his or her experience of intellectual activity to a desired level, which varies depending on who we are. When a person of faith has spent more time thinking than he or she likes, the individual can embrace religious teachings as literal truths or revelations. When a person of faith is bored, the individual can increase intellectual activity by reading or pondering theology.

THE STRIVING FOR NOURISHMENT

People differ not only in how much they usually like to eat but also in the symbolic value eating has for them. Hearty Eaters consume large quantities of food, which they view symbolically as nourishment. They may take pride in their refined taste, knowledge of food, or cooking skills. On the other hand, Light Eaters consume

Table 7-3

Religion and Eating	
INCREASES EATING	**DECREASES EATING**
Positive Body Attitude	Negative Body Attitude
Food is God-given	Gluttony is Sin
Feasts	Fasts
Eucharist	God has No Body
Dietary Laws	Dietary Laws

relatively small quantities of food, which some view symbolically as healthy living or as self-discipline. Table 7-3 identifies some of the religious beliefs and practices that encourage or discourage eating.

The Judeo-Christian religions give the faithful a number of reasons to value the body and to satisfy its needs. These religions teach that God created the human body, and while he was on Earth, Jesus had a body and ate. As the Bible states, "Do you not know that your body is a temple of the Holy Spirit, who is in you, whom you have received from God....Therefore honor God with your body" (1 Corinthians. 6:19–20).

On the other hand, Christianity also views the pleasures of the body negatively insofar as they are distractions away from spiritual pursuits. The Roman Catholic Church regards gluttony as a sin. These teachings support the values of Light Eaters.

Hearty Eaters, of course, enjoy religious feasts, which are held on certain holidays, usually as part of festivals commemorating an important historical event, person, or change of season. The Pentecost is one of the prominent feasts in Christianity commemorating the descent of the Holy Spirit upon the disciples of Christ. The Jewish Purim celebrates the deliverance of the Jewish people from an evil Persian plot. Hearty Eaters also appreciate the practice of serving food after Sunday services. Southern churches are known for lavish after-the-service dinners on Sunday, laden with fried chicken, biscuits, and heavy desserts, or potluck Wednesday night dinners in the fellowship hall. On the other hand, fasting is a religious practice that reinforces the values of Light Eaters.

The sacrament of Holy Communion in the Christian tradition involves eating and is generally considered to be a reenactment of Christ's Last Supper—the final meal Jesus shared with his disciples before his arrest. When he gave them bread and wine, he said, "This is my body... this is my blood."

Many religions invoke strict dietary rules that encourage the faithful to satisfy the need for sustenance in moderation. For the faithful, obedience to these laws imbues eating with religious meaning and significance. The Jewish Kashrut (which identifies when foods are "kosher" or "fit" to eat) prohibits eating pork, among other things, and requires that meat and milk not be eaten together. Muslims also are forbidden to eat pork. Buddhists refrain from eating meat, although some eat fish. Hindus are prohibited from eating beef and discouraged from drinking alcohol.

In summary, religions help the faithful manage eating habits in ways most meaningful to them. Some religious beliefs and practices increase food consumption and/or express the values of Hearty Eaters, while other religious beliefs and practices decrease food consumption and/or express the values of Light Eaters. Each person of faith can use these religious phenomena to help manage his or her consumption to a desired level. When a person of faith eats too much, he or she can fast, embrace religious dietary rules, focus on gluttony as sin, or turn to religion to bolster self-discipline. When a person of faith is hungry, he or she can attend feasts or think of food as divine-given sustenance.

THE STRIVING FOR FAMILY LIFE

Individuals vary in how strongly they experience the desire to raise a family. Family-Focused people have a high or strong need; they may make raising a family a life purpose and tend to organize their lives around the needs of their children. Adult-Focused people have a low or weak need and may experience children as burdensome or find excuses to be away from home. A few go so far as to abandon their children.

Table 7-4

Religion and Feelings of Family Love

ENCOURAGES FAMILY VALUES	DISCOURAGES FAMILY VALUES
God as Father, Son	God Before Family
Sanctity of Marriage	
Congregation helps families in need	

Table 7-4 identifies some of the religious beliefs and practices that encourage or discourage family life. On balance the Judeo-Christian religions support Family-Focused people and offer less support for Adult-Focused people.

The Christian conception of divinity in family terms—such as "God the Father" and "God the Son"—validates the values of Family-Focused people. In Catholicism the priest is called "father" and members of various religious orders are called "sisters" and "brothers." The clergy encourage the faithful to think of the congregation as their family. The clergy bless parenthood from the pulpit. Catholicism's prohibition against birth control strengthens its message that sex is for having children and not for pleasure.

The Bible encourages responsible parenting (Proverbs 22:6; Ephesians 6:4), and it instructs parents to love their children, provide for them, and raise them in a religious household. Local churches encourage families to pray together.

The Bible teaches that marriage is a sacred duty and family life is holy. Husbands are to honor their wives and make them happy, and wives are to willingly obey their husbands. Children are to honor and obey their parents, to learn from their parents, and to take of care of them when they become elderly or sick.

Since the Judeo-Christian religions propagate themselves primarily through families, churches and synagogues do what they can to support families through difficult times. The clergy counsel families through experiences with death, hard times, relationship troubles, alcoholism, or difficult or rebellious children. Churches encourage the congregation to help out a family who has fallen on hard times; they may organize, for example, efforts to rebuild a house that was destroyed by fire or a storm.

The Judeo-Christian religions have few beliefs and practices that decrease interest in family life. One notable exception is the teaching that God comes first even before family, as expressed in the Biblical example of Abraham's willingness to obey God and sacrifice his son Isaac. From a psychological standpoint, some devout people who are Adult-Focused could embrace this principle to find meaning in their lack of interest in marrying and/or raising children. It might inspire some to join a monastery to avoid family life.

In conclusion, the Judeo-Christian religions encourage family life and express the values of Family-Focused people. Other than teaching that God comes first, the Judeo-Christian religions offer few beliefs and practices that discourage family life or express the values of Adult-Focused people.

THE STRIVING FOR CHARACTER

The basic desire for honor motivates adherence to a moral code of conduct. All religions are concerned with such codes. They all distinguish between good versus evil, and right versus wrong. They all teach a moral code of conduct to children, and all encourage moral behavior in adults.

Many religions suggest specific codes of moral conduct to guide righteous living. The Ten Commandments is, of course, the moral code God gave Moses on Mount Sinai. The Golden Rule instructs the faithful to treat others as they would have others treat them. Confucius (Analects XV.24) taught, "Never impose on others what you would not choose for yourself." The Bible says, "Love your neighbor as yourself " (Leviticus 19:18) and "Do to no one what you yourself dislike" (Mark 12:31).

The Islamic moral code prohibits gambling, sexual promiscuity, and the use of intoxicants. The leaders of the early Catholic Church devoted considerable energy to moral typologies, specifying exactly what the faithful should do and think, and what they should refrain from doing and thinking. One such list is familiar

Table 7-5

Religion and Honor

INSPIRES/EXPANDS HONOR	IMPEDES/REDUCES HONOR
4 Cardinal Virtues	7 Deadly Sins
Ten Commandments	Impure Thoughts
Forgiveness/Penitence	Awareness of Sin
God as Perfect Goodness	Devil as Pure Evil
Loyalty to Tribe/Ancestors	
Karma	

to us today as the seven "mortal" or "deadly" sins: lust, gluttony, greed, sloth, wrath, envy, and pride. Lists of desirable practices were compiled as well, such as the four Cardinal virtues of prudence, temperance, courage, and justice

Individuals differ considerably in how concerned they are with morality, honor, and character. Righteous people place a high, above-average value on honor, but Expedient people place a low, below-average value. Some Expedient people may profess allegiance to certain moral values but behave differently when it is in their self-interest to do so.

Table 7-5 shows some significant religious beliefs and practices that help people manage the basic desire for honor. Some of these phenomena express the values of Righteous people, while others express the values of Expedient people.

Soren Kierkegaard (2013/1844), the father of philosophical existentialism, thought that religion can make us feel less honorable by increasing our awareness of sin. Writing in her unpublished doctoral dissertation at The Ohio State University, Patricia Yoder discussed how her religion made her more aware of sin. She wrote,

> From these tales and my own vivid imagination, I developed a concept of a God who could see and was concerned about everything I did and thought and who would send me to hell for all eternity for any infraction of a rule (pp. 5-6).

On the other hand, the Judeo-Christian religions teach that God forgives people who practice sincere penitence. Roman Catholicism empowers priests to forgive people who confess their sins. These practices help to increase the sense of honor by making people feel less sinful.

Righteous people may be encouraged by the conceptions of God as perfectly moral and as a giver of moral rules to humanity. They may aim to imitate God's moral purity, even though they believe their efforts are nothing compared to his perfection.

On the other hand, Expedient people may be encouraged by the idea of a supernatural being, variously called the "devil" or "Satan," who personifies evil and opposes God. Allegiance to God typically increases feelings of honor, while allegiance to the devil typically decreases such feelings.

Some eastern religions have a belief in karma, which is a moral natural law of cause and effect. It says that your current status in life—how happy you are, how serene, how relaxed—depends on the sum total of your past deeds and wants both in this life and in past lives. It implies that, over the long haul, no deed is without consequence, either in this life or in a reincarnation, even if that is not apparent or understood now. It provides a message to the wicked that they cannot escape the consequences of their immoral actions, and if it seems otherwise it is because they are ignorant of what will happen to them in the future, perhaps in a future rein- carnated life. On the other hand, the righteous are reassured that, eventually, their good deeds will be rewarded.

Honor motivates loyalty to parents and ancestors. Typically children honor their parents and ancestors by embracing their reli- gion. This theme can be traced all the way back to when people lived in tribes in the wilderness. In those days deities were passion- ately biased in favor of tribes that worshipped them. Jews, for example, promised loyalty to Yahweh, who gave them a moral code to obey as a test of their loyalty, and in exchange he protected them. The theme is played out on a much smaller scale in families where children initially embrace the religion of their parents out of loyalty to them, and in exchange they earn the favor of their parents' protection, and the right to be "honored" within their ethnic group or religion as "good" children. This message is taught from the pulpit, expressed in the Bible, and reinforced by the congregation. "I am God, the God of your father," Yahweh says to Moses (Genesis 46:3). By marrying within their religion or at least practicing it as adults, the faithful increase satisfaction of their basic desire for honor.

Judaism and Islam are monotheistic, which historically had distinguished them from the polytheistic religions. Psychologically, it was an act of loyalty for early Jews and Muslims to embrace monotheism. Jews pray, "Hear, O Israel, The Lord is Our God, The Lord is One." Muslims pray, "There is no God but God and Mohammad is his prophet."

In summary, religion addresses the needs of both Righteous and Expedient personality types and everybody in between them. People who seek to increase their honor can do so by embracing the behaviors their religion defines as moral or by reducing the behaviors their religion defines as immoral. Those who seek to reduce their sense of honor can do so by becoming more aware of their sins, temptations, character flaws, and disloyalties.

THE STRIVING FOR SOCIAL JUSTICE

The basic desire for idealism determines how inclined we are to lend a helping hand to strangers in need. Idealists, who have a strong basic desire, include altruistic people, humanitarians, do-gooders, and philanthropists. They may serve as volunteers fighting inner-city poverty, scientists seeking the cure for a deadly disease, or political leaders dedicated to world peace.

Realists, who have a weak basic desire for idealism, tolerate social injustice as a necessary evil almost impossible to do away with. These individuals find excuses for not becoming involved; they look the other way and may be pragmatic or hard-nosed.

Some of the religious phenomena that address idealism are shown in Table 7-6.

Table 7-6
Religion and Social Justice

ENCOURAGES COMPASSION	DISCOURAGES COMPASSION
God is Compassionate, Blesses Poor	God Appears to Tolerate Social Injustice
Charity (God's Work)	Intolerance and Bigotry
Religious Freedom/Tolerance	Religious Wars
Role Models/World Peace	Negative Role Models/ Molestation, Abuse

The Judeo-Christian conception of God as social justice inspires Idealists and encourages the faithful toward acts of charity. Religion further encourages charitable activities from the pulpit. In many large western countries religious charities provide food and shelter for the poor, orphaned, and homeless. Charity is an important value of many religions.

Muslims have a personal responsibility to ease poverty and eliminate inequality. The Koran exhorts them to feed the hungry and to spend on those in need. Each Muslim is required to spend 2.5% of his wealth for the benefit of the poor or needy. Buddhism teaches that material possessions cannot be taken from one life to another; individuals, however, can enhance their own karma—which would improve their future lives—through charitable giving.

Religious intolerance and bigotry express the values of Realists. History has recorded many religious wars. The Salem witch trials, and the Spanish Inquisition, also stand out as extraordinary examples of religion at its worst. Karen Armstrong (1993) noted that the rise of monotheism was historically associated with intolerance and with religious wars.

The clergy offer a number of positive examples of people who inspire idealism, especially among young adults. In my student days at Yale, for example, our chaplin was William Sloane Coffin, the former CIA agent who was a prominent anti-war activist and leader in the fight for racial equality. Coffin used his pulpit as a platform for like-minded crusaders, hosting the Rev. Martin Luther King Jr.,

Archbishop Desmond Tutu, and many others who were themselves positive religious role models.

On the other hand, the clergy also offer examples of people who inspire realistic attitudes toward mankind. Some Catholics were demoralized by reports of priests who sexually molested young boys in their congregations. Misconduct on the part of the clergy has the effect of encouraging the attitude that sin will never be eradicated from the world.

In summary, religion addresses the needs of both Idealists and Realists and everybody in between them. To help the faithful manage their experiences of justice and compassion to the psychological level most meaningful to them, religion offers a number of beliefs and practices—such as charity and the conception of God as just—that increase compassion for others and validate the values of Idealists. Religion also offers beliefs and practices—such as God's apparent tolerance of injustice, religious wars, inquisitions, and bigotry—that decrease compassion and support the values of Realists. Each person of faith can use these religious phenomena to manage his or her experience of idealism to a desired level, which varies depending on who we are.

THE STRIVING FOR PERSONAL FREEDOM

Although we sometimes feel uncomfortable having to depend on others to meet our needs, being on our own also can be frightening. How we strike the balance depends on who we are. Independent-minded people, who have a strong basic desire, like to make their own decisions and do things their way. They do not wish to rely on anybody to meet their needs, perhaps not even on God. On the other hand, Interdependent people, who have a weak basic desire, dislike being on their own and look to others for support and help. They are comforted by images of a supportive deity.

Table 7-7 shows some of the religious beliefs and practices that address the basic desire for independence.

There are several ways of presenting God, and these have implications for how independent or interdependent we feel. The

Table 7-7
Religion and Independence

ENCOURAGES AUTONOMY	DISCOURAGES AUTONOMY
God as Self-Sufficient	Divinity as Unity, Mystical Union, Infinity
Finitude/Body	Transcendence/Mind, Soul
Islam: Unique Individuality, Buddhism: Soul Searching	Community Support
God Gave me Free Will	Petition Prayers
	Buddhism: Fetters

Judeo-Christian concept of God as self-sufficient may inspire some people of faith toward independence. The suggestion is that it is good to be self-sufficient, or this would not be a divine attribute. On the other hand, the mystic's conception of God as the unity underlying all reality may decrease the sense of independence. Mystics teach us to understand others as extensions of selves. If self-sufficiency is an illusion, then surely it is unwise to value and aim for it.

The religious concept of transcendence decreases the sense of being an individual on our own in a vast universe. As expressed by the brilliant theologian Reinhold Niebuhr (1949), we seek to escape from the constant need to take care of our bodies for survival. We look to transcend the body and gain greater degree of existence.

On the other hand, some theologians have embraced autonomy and individuality. Islamic scholar Muhammad Iqbal supported the value of autonomy with his teachings concerning the uniqueness of the self. He wrote, "All life is individual, there is no such thing as universal life, God Himself is an individual, He is the Most Unique individual" (Smith, 1991, p. 240).

Buddhists believe that each individual must do his or her own soul searching and not just follow or listen to others or to authority. The Pali Sutta instructs its followers , "Work out your own salvation. Do not depend on others." Enlightened individuals only point out the way for others to work out their own salvation. The Soto

Zen teach, "Do not walk in the footsteps of the masters—seek only what they sought" (Smith, 1991, p. 97).

Buddhists believe that fetters—such as rites and rituals, sensual desire, ill will, conceit, and ignorance—decrease independence by connecting us to an endless cycle of birth, death, and rebirth. In striving for nirvana, Buddhists seek liberation from fetters and a state of not needing anything.

The religious doctrine of free will increases our psychological sense of independence. Theologians encourage the faithful to think of themselves as free to make their own moral decisions and to determine their own life. They recognize freedom to decide between religion or atheism; to behave morally or not; and to love God or to turn away from him. Such freedom of choice is essential if people are later to be held responsible for their actions and decisions. After all, it would make no sense to blame someone for rejecting God if the person did not freely choose to have done so and could not have chosen otherwise.

Many larger churches offer social services and other community supports for their members. These reduce the perception that one is on one's own, or independent. The local priest takes a personal interest in church members and is sympathetic when an individual or family is challenged. Members of the congregation tend to be supportive of each other. In total, these practices can add up to significant social support for any *Inter*dependent person who dislikes being on his or her own.

In summary, the basic desire of independence motivates self-reliance and how much freedom we need. Independent-minded people seek a relatively high degree of self-reliance, while Interdependent people seek a relatively low degree. Religion addresses the needs of both personality types and everybody in between them. It offers some beliefs and practices—such as the presentation of God as self-sufficient and a belief in free will—that validate the values of Independent-minded people. It also offers other beliefs and practices—such as mystical union and a church community—that validate the values of Interdependent people. Each person of faith can use these religious phenomena to manage his or her experience of freedom to a desired level, which varies depending on who we are. When a person of faith has the feeling of being on one's own, he or she can draw comfort in believing that God is ready to provide assistance if needed. When a person of faith feels trapped by his or her dependency on a sick body, he or she can embrace mystical visions of unity.

THE STRIVING FOR STRUCTURE

People differ in how much structure they need. Organized people seek high degrees of structure in both their environment and their daily activities. They typically like to organize, plan, and write "to do" lists, because all these activities increase structure. On the other hand, Spontaneous people seek relatively low degrees of structure and have a tendency to "follow their nose". They may be poorly organized, sloppy, untidy, and chronically late.

Table 7-8 shows some of the religious beliefs and practices that address the basic desire for order.

The conception of God as immortal provides the faithful with a reassuring psychological sense of permanence and, thus, order. No matter what happens to the physical universe—and even if a future collision of galaxies were to annihilate Earth—the faithful believe there will always be God, and he will always be the same.

Table 7-8

Religion and Structure

ENCOURAGES ORDERLINESS	DISCOURAGES ORDERLINESS
Divine Immortality/ Immortality of Soul	Apocalypse
Immortality of Soul	Mortality of Body
Biblical Stories e.g., Babel, Chaos	Acceptance of Change
Ritual	
Samsara	
Fate	

Although we conceive of God as perfect order, he has used chaos to do his will. The story of Babel validates the values of Organized People by casting chaos in an unfavorable light.

> *Therefore is the name of it called Babel; because the Lord did there confound the language of all the earth: and from thence did the Lord scatter them abroad upon the face of all the earth (Genesis 11:9).*

Some ancient creation myths told stories about gods imposing order on flux. In the ancient Babylonian poem "Enuma Elish," for example, the gods create the universe from a formless, primordial mass that resembled a swamp, or a sloppy mess where everything lacks boundary, definition, and identity. The poem describes creation as a struggle against the forces of chaos. The Bible, moreover, informs us that God created the universe in an orderly manner. All this supports the values of Organized people. On the other hand, believing in an apocalypse reduces the sense of an orderly universe. In his book *Jesus, Interrupted,* Biblical scholar Bart Ehrman (2010) wrote that the historical Jesus was likely a "Jewish apocalyptic prophet" (p. 156).

Apocalypticists teach that God will soon destroy the world, raise the dead, and judge everyone.

All religions encourage the practice of rituals, which are symbolic acts that are repeatedly performed over and over again. Rituals give people a sense of order by enhancing sameness in their lives and making their futures more predictable and familiar. Examples of religious rituals include daily prayer, the weekly Sabbath, rites of passage (e.g., confirmation or bar mitzvah), the observance of the same holidays every year (e.g., Christmas, Easter, Chanukah), celebrations (e.g., as of the harvest, for example), and certain expressions of respect (for instance, the genuflecting of Catholics before the cross).

Buddhism teaches that permanence is an illusion and we must learn to accept continual change. This teaching decreases the psychological sense of order by valuing the acceptance of change.

The doctrine of mind-body dualism is relevant to our desire for order. The human body, of course, is perishable from decay, disease, or injury. All we need to do to decrease our sense of a predictable, unchanging future is to reflect on our mortality and how illness can interrupt even the best-laid plans. In contrast, the faithful can increase their sense of order by thinking about the indestructible and permanent nature of the human soul.

Some eastern religions believe in the Samsara. In Hinduism and Buddhism, the Samsara is an endless passage through cycles of life, death, and rebirth, Thinking about the Samara probably increases the psychological sense of orderliness. No matter what happens the faithful believe Samara itself continues on.

Some people believe that God has a plan for everyone. This idea implies that things do not happen to us chaotically or sense-lessly but in accordance with a divine purpose. Beliefs in fate increase the psychological sense of an orderly universe.

In summary, the basic desire for order motivates people to impose form and structure on their life and their environment. Organized people seek relatively high degrees of order, while Spontaneous people seek relatively low degrees. To help the faithful manage their experiences of order to the psychological level most meaningful to them, religion offers a number of beliefs and prac-tices—notably the conception of God as eternal and ceremonial rituals—that increase the psychological sense of order. Religion also offers other beliefs and practices—notably the Christian teaching of apocalypse and the Buddhist teaching of the need to embrace change—that decrease the psychological sense of order. Each person of faith can use these religious phenomena to manage his or her experience of order to a desired level, which varies depending on who we are. When a person of faith is uncomfortable with what he or she perceives to be chaos or rapid change, the indi-vidual can practice religious rituals or contemplate divine eternity to restore a psychological sense of order. When a person of faith feels constrained or bored by life's routines, the individual may vary how he or she performs religious rituals or may contemplate the uncertainty of the future and the possibility of apocalypse.

THE STRIVING FOR VITALITY

Active people have a strong need for physical activity. They are typically fit, perky, energetic, and possibly athletic. In contrast, Inactive people have a weak need for physical activity. They are typically lackadaisical, listless, lethargic, and sedentary.

Table 7-9 shows some important religious beliefs and practices addressing the need for physical activity.

Images of strong or vigorous gods can inspire the faithful to exercise their bodies in imitation of divinity. The ancient Greeks, for example, admired physical strength as something glorious and divine. Muscular strength is an attribute of the Homeric gods: Zeus is the strongest of these gods. Although the Judeo-Christian God does not have a body and, thus, has no muscles, he is conceived of as being "Almighty," or infinitely strong. His whispers are thunderous, he can move mountains or even planets, and there is no force strong enough to stop him.

Samson is the Biblical character best identified with God-given muscular strength. Although things did not work out well for him, his legendary strength still inspires some Israelites. When Active people contemplate Samson's very impressive strength, their values

Table 7-9

Religion and Physical Activity

ENCOURAGES EXERCISE	DISCOURAGES EXERCISE
God as Almighty	Sabbath
Biblical Characters	
Body as God-Given	
Ceremonial Dances	
Religion and Athletics	

are reinforced. This encourages them to imitate Samson as a role model and develop their own strength.

As was previously noted, the Bible encourages the faithful to take care of the body because it is God-given. This attitude may inspire some to exercise and be fit. It imbues physical workouts with additional religious significance. By taking care of our bodies, we not only are staying healthy but also are fulfilling an obligation to God. The Sabbath is a day of rest set aside each week in imitation of the day God rested. It imbues rest with divine significance. It encourages the faithful to regulate or manage how physically active they are and not to overdo it.

Dancing is a common form of devotion used globally to celebrate and praise God. In Judaism dance is mentioned frequently in the Hebrew Bible Old but not in the Christian New Testament. Religious ceremonial dancing, of course, increases physical activity and supports the values of Active people.

Some religious schools have athletic teams. Catholic high schools and colleges in the United States, for example, tend to be athletic powerhouses. "The Fighting Irish," as the University of Notre Dame's football team is known, has inspired numerous Catholic athletes. Sandy Koufax, the best pitcher in baseball when I was a boy, was a role model for Jewish athletes.

In summary, the basic desire for physical activity motivates muscle exercise and associated values such as fitness, strength, and vitality. Active people seek a relatively high degree of physical activity, while Inactive people seek a relatively low degree. When a person of faith wants to increase physical activity, the individual can participate in a church-sponsored fitness program. When a person of faith feels tired, he or she might view the Sabbath as God's blessing of rest.

THE STRIVING FOR POWER

This is a basic desire for influence of will. Assertive people, who have a strong basic desire, typically embrace leadership or "dominant" roles. In contrast, Nonassertive people, who have a weak basic

Table 7-10

Religion and Power (Will)	
INCREASES VALUATION OF POWER	**DECREASES VALUATION OF POWER**
Omnipotent Deity, Miracles	Surrender, Obey God
Creation	Disciples
Praise for Hard Work	
God as Lord	Assistant Roles in Church Hierarchy
Power of Faith	
Leadership Roles in Church Hierarchy	

desire, typically embrace the role of assistant or onlooker. Onlookers are reluctant to intervene, give advice to others, or make suggestions.

Assertive people usually value competence, hard work, and achievement, while Nonassertive people value life-work balance and a moderate pace of work. Table 7-10 shows some religious phenomena that address the basic desire for power.

The values of Assertive people are supported by presentations of the divine as all-powerful. Islam presents God as possessing awesome, fear-inspiring power. The Judeo-Christian God is conceived of as omnipotent. He is the ultimate leader, or Lord, with absolute authority. The Bible tells us that he only has to will something for it to happen: "He doeth according to his will in the army of heaven, and among the inhabitants of the earth: and none can stay his hand, or say unto him, What dost Thou?" (Daniel 4:35).

Religions have presented the divine as possessing many different powers. God created the universe and everything in it. He can bring to pass whatever he pleases, "God said, Let there be...and it was so" (Genesis 1). God can heal the sick or raise the dead. To the leper he said, "I Will, be thou clean, and immediately his leprosy was cleansed" (Matthew 8:3). The prophets were needed to mediate human contact with God because unmediated contact would be too overpowering.

Presentations of the divine as powerful validate the desires and values of Assertive people. If God is a great leader, then shouldn't they embrace their own ambitions to lead? If God is all-powerful, should they not exert their own powers as fully as they can? If God is creator, should they not create and build as well? In these and similar ways, God's power encourages people to assert their own will. The Bible says, "Finally, be strong in the Lord and in the strength of his might" (Ephesians 6:10).

On the other hand, some Nonassertive people may see religious submission and obedience as validating their own desire to suppress their will. Psychologically, submission to God resembles the surrender in love, in which the subjection of the will can be total. It leads to inner peace because of the lack of any cross-purpose.

Religious people can satisfy their psychological need for power at least partially through faith in God. Here are two Biblical references to strength from faith: "It is God that girdeth me with strength, and maketh my way perfect" (Psalms 18:32). "I will love thee, O Lord, my strength" (Psalms 18:1).

Hinduism blesses ambition and worldly success as one of four legitimate goals of life. It acknowledges the need for respect based on achievement. It cautions, however, against becoming overly ambitious and too extreme in the pursuit of materialism and world success. These teachings express the values of Assertive people.

The Bible offers a number of proverbs intended to discourage laziness (sloth). Typical of these is Proverbs 10:4, "He becometh poor that dealeth with a slack hand, but the hand of the diligent maketh rich." The view of sloth as a vice expresses the values of Assertive people.

The Bible includes outstanding examples of important people in the roles of helper and assistant. The disciples, for example, followed and assisted Jesus. According to the theory of 16 basic desires, the Biblical significance of the disciples validates the values of Nonassertive individuals.

Church administration offers both Assertive and Nonassertive people opportunities to satisfy their basic desire for power. Assertive individuals might pursue leadership opportunities in their own congregation or religious denomination. There are many outstanding religious leaders who could serve as role models for any churchgoer with leadership tendencies. Scholars have studied the leadership styles of Jesus, Moses, King Solomon, Paul, and many others. On the other hand, local churches also provide many opportunities for Nonassertive churchgoers to assume assistant and supportive roles in their congregation or church hierarchy.

In summary, the basic desire for power motivates people to express their will to make a difference. Assertive people seek relatively high degrees of power, while Nonassertive people seek relatively low degrees. To address the needs of both personality types and everybody in between them, religion provides some experiences that strengthen the expression of will, and others that suppress it, so that people of faith can combine them as they desire, picking and choosing those most comfortable for them, while setting aside or ignoring those they regard as less meaningful. Each individual is free to strike the balance most meaningful to him or her.

THE STRIVING FOR ROMANCE

People differ significantly in how much time and effort they devote to romance. Sensual people, who have a strong desire, typically seek frequent sexual experiences and may have an above-average appreciation for beauty. Some brag about their romantic exploits. Ascetic people, who have a weak desire, typically seek sexual experiences only infrequently. Some brag about their self-restraint. Sensual people typically embrace romantic love and beauty, while Ascetic people typically embrace abstinence, plainness, and drabness.

Table 7-11 shows some religious phenomena that address the need for romance.

Some religious phenomena imbue romantic love with divine significance and, thus, support the values of Sensual people. The

Table 7-11
Religion and Romance

ENCOURAGES ROMANCE	DISCOURAGES ROMANCE
Goddesses	Original Sin/Lust as Sin
Sexual Imagery, Fertility Rites	Celibacy, Asceticism
Holy Union (Marriage)	Conservative Attitudes

gods and goddesses of ancient Rome, Greece, and India, for example, married and had sex. The Roman goddess for love is Venus; her Hindu counterpart is Parvati, who is the second wife of the god Shiva. Sexually explicit sculptures were located in ancient Hindu temples.

The Judeo-Christian God is male and patriarchic, and although he has no divine wife, in some orders nuns think of themselves as married to him.

The use of sexual imagery in ancient religions includes fertility rites, which involved actual or symbolic sex. Although aimed at making the female earth fertile, these rites were motivated by sexual desire. They included dancing, wine, and in some societies, sex without prohibition. A common theme was that mother earth is female, and the sun is male, and the action of the sun on the earth symbolizes sexual intercourse.

Some Christian theologians viewed romantic passion as a temptation that distracts people from spiritual life. St. Paul's words to the Romans were: "Put on the Lord Jesus Christ and make no provision for the flesh and its lusts" (Armstrong, 1993, p. 120). Priests are celibate, monks make a vow of chastity, and in some religions monks are castrated (becoming eunuchs) for the sake of Heaven. The Catholic doctrine of original sin suggests that child bearing is God's punishment to women for sex between Adam and Eve.

The Judeo-Christian religions have frowned on sex outside of marriage and regard adultery as a sin. Moses interpreted the covenant to mean no intermarriage and no social mixing with goyim non-Jews. Catholicism encourages sex for the purpose of having children and raising a family. Judaism regards appropriate sexual behavior as a mitzvah, a sacred human activity potentially imbued with holiness.

The Judeo-Christian religions are male-dominated even though women tend to be more religious than men. Historically, some religions have portrayed women as temptresses who should be resisted. As Saint Augustine put it, "What is the difference whether it is a wife or a mother, it is still Eve the temptress that we must be aware of in any woman" (cited in Armstrong, 2009, p. 124).

Hinduism recognizes pleasure as one of the four legitimate ends of life. It also teaches that pleasure is not the only end in life and encourages the use of common sense when pursuing hedonism.

In summary, the basic desire for romance motivates people to have sex and appreciate beauty. Sensual people seek relatively high degrees of romance, while Ascetic people seek relatively low degrees. To help the faithful balance experiences of sensuality and asceticism to the psychological level most meaningful to them as individuals, religion offers a number of beliefs and practices— notably the concept of holy union and use of sexual imagery—that increase sexual desire and romance. Religion also offers other beliefs and practices—notably asceticism and the concept of passion as sin—that discourage sexual desire and romance. Further, many religions encourage moderation and the satisfaction of romantic desires within the context of holy matrimony.

THE STRIVING FOR COLLECTIONS

People experience the basic desire for saving at various degrees of strength. Collectors are "pack rats," or people who hate throwing things away thinking they might come in handy in the future. Many (but not all) Collectors are frugal. Non-collectors tend to throw the things they use away rather than save them.

Table 7-12 shows some of the religious phenomena that address the basic desire for saving.

The faithful may collect relics or various religious items of one type or another. Some religions have stores where Collectors can

Table 7-12

Religion and Saving

ENCOURAGES SAVING	DISCOURAGES SAVING
Relics. Icons. Mementos	Jesus's Parable of Rich Man
Bible Stories	

purchase such items. The churches themselves collect, or at least preserve for posterity, important works of sculpture and art.

The Bible story of "seven years of plenty, seven years of famine" explains the importance of collection. Pharaoh dreamt he stood by the river and watched seven fat cows feed on the meadow, and then he saw seven lean cows come by and they ate the fat cows (Genesis 41). After a number of dreams with a similar theme, Joseph interpreted them to mean that Egypt would experience seven years of plenty followed by seven years of famine. So Egypt gathered its crop during the years of plenty and stored it to feed the people during the years of famine. The story shows us the importance of saving during good times to prepare for bad times.

In an unrelated story that shows the pitfalls of excessive saving, Jesus told the parable of a rich man with such an abundance of crop, he planned to build a bigger barn so he could store his crops and not have to work in the future. But God said to him, "You fool this very night you are going to be dead. Who will then benefit by all those things that you have stored for yourself?" Jesus said, "This is what happens to all those who hoard riches for themselves but who are actually not rich in the eye of God."

In summary, the basic desire for saving motivates people to collect. Although religion offers relics and bible stories that discuss collecting, actually it seems that little in religion addresses this basic desire.

THE STRIVING FOR BELONGING

People vary considerably in how much social life they want. Extroverts are gregarious people who enjoy being around others.

Table 7-13

Religion and Social Life	
ENCOURAGES RICH SOCIAL LIFE	**DISCOURAGES RICH SOCIAL LIFE**
God/Angels as Friends	Impersonal Presentations of God
Belonging to Faith Community	Hermits, Private Meditations, Retreats
Festivals	Social Life as Fetter

They tend to be affable, friendly, and outgoing. Introverts like to keep to themselves. They may be shy, distant, or private.

Table 7-13 shows some of the religious phenomena that address the basic desire for social contact.

The faithful imagine God in different ways. One tradition refers to God as a personal deity with whom a relationship is possible. Some people, for example, think of God or his angels as friends. According to our theory of 16 strivings for God, Extroverts may interpret personal relationships with spiritual beings as a validation of the value of fellowship.

Another tradition suggests a less personal, more businesslike deity. Some believers, for example, think of God as remote and probably not paying much attention to them as individuals. According to our theory of 16 strivings for God, these businesslike presentations of God should appeal to Introverts. Aristotle's Prime Mover, for example, has no feelings, pays no attention to us, and neither listens to our prayers nor provides us with emotional support.

Some religions value solitary lifestyles. The religious hermit, or person who lives alone away from society, lives a recognized form of spiritual life. *The Rule* of Saint Benedict recognizes hermits in its typology of four kinds of monks.

Although monastic life is communal, monks do not party and are known for being serious people. This is consistent with the values of Introverts. In monasteries monks and nuns devote many hours to private prayer and meditation.

As was previously noted, the Buddha taught that social attachments are potential obstacles on the path toward enlightenment. This attitude stands in sharp contrast to the Christian concept of fellowship and to Durkheim's theory of religion as communal bonding. The Buddhist view expresses the values of Introverts.

Emile Durkheim (1965/1915) suggested that religion is the cement of the community, or the means by which people turn from the everyday concerns in which they are enmeshed to a common devotion to sacred things. He referred to a church as a "moral community" (Durkheim, 1965/1915). Membership in a church gives people a sense of belonging.

The social aspects of religion are varied and numerous. Many churches sponsor outings, picnics, trips, dances for young people, and bingo or other social activities for elderly people. The members of a local church pray together, sing together, and watch each other's children grow up. They have many opportunities to socialize, such as after-service meals that offer time for people to keep up with each other.

The following passages from the Bible encourage fellowship:

* Keep on loving each other as brothers (Hebrews 13:1).
* Show proper respect to everyone: Love the brotherhood of believers, fear God, honor the king (1PE 2:17).
* Finally, all of you, live in harmony with one another; be sympathetic, love as brothers, be compassionate and humble (1Peter 3:8).

In summary, the basic desire for social contact motivates people to make friends, join groups, and have fun. Extroverts seek an active social life, while Introverts seek a quiet, serious life with few friends and minimal social experiences. To help the faithful manage their social experiences to the psychological level most meaningful to them, religion offers a number of beliefs and practices—notably fellowship among church members and the conception of spiritual beings as personal friends—that express the values of Extroverts. It also offers other beliefs and practices—notably impersonal deities, retreats, and private meditations—that express the values of Introverts. Each person of faith can combine these religious phenomena to manage his or her social experiences to a desired level or balance, which varies depending on who the person is. When a person of faith feels lonely, he or she can imagine God or angels as friends. When a person of faith feels a need for solitude, he or she can go on a retreat or meditate and pray in private.

THE STRIVING FOR SIGNIFICANCE

People vary in how important status is to them. Formal people, who have a strong basic desire, tend to be impressed with marks of social distinction and with prestigious possessions, including class, titles, and wealth. They may be motivated to embrace the mannerisms, dress, and habits of prestigious or wealthy people. Typically it is important to them to be associated with the "right" people. They may be materialistic, patrician, formal, and/or dignified.

In contrast, Informal people, who have a weak basic desire, are unimpressed with high social class. They may believe it is wrong to admire someone just because he or she happens to be born into a certain family or is wealthy. They may be informal in their manner and inclined to identify with ordinary folks. Some may "thumb their nose" at proprietary; they may not care what others think of them. These individuals tend to be down-to-earth, unceremonious, and egalitarian.

Table 7-14 shows some of the religious phenomena that address the basic desire for social status.

Divinity is the highest imaginable status. Its attributes include: immortal, eternal, and indestructible, each of which indicates a high status.

Hinduism presents three major or primary gods—Brahma, Vishnu, and Shiva—and a number of avatars and deities of lesser status. This feature of Hinduism implies that status is such an important quality it applies even to the gods.

The belief that humans are divinely created makes us important and special, which are indicators of our status. The Christian belief

Table 7-14
Religion and Social Status

ENHANCES IMPORTANCE OF STATUS	DIMINISHES IMPORTANCE OF STATUS
Humans Divinely Created	Equality Before God
Hindu Caste System	Vows of Poverty/Humility
Chosen People, Covenant	White Garments
Sacred	Expensive Churches
	Profane
	Insignificance vs. Nature, God

that God sent his only son to Earth elevates the status of human beings. We reason that since God has paid so much attention to us, we must be important.

Although theologians debate exactly what it means to believe that Jews were chosen, psychologists can recognize the Jewish convenant as an expression of the value of status.

The idea that all people are equal before God expresses the values of Informal people. Islam teaches that all people are equal in the sight of the Lord. Muslim pilgrims remove attire and don two simple white garments so that everyone—both prince and pauper—wears the same clothes and are undivided before God.

In Christianity, God and church bless the poor: "Blessed are you poor, for yours is the kingdom of God" (Luke 6:20). When the highest imaginable status, Christ, blesses people of low status, the poor, one of the implications is that social class and wealth are false indicators of a person's worth and true importance. Some people look at a poor person and see a "nobody," but God sees a future king. Some people look at a commoner and see an "unimportant" person, but God sees a blessed soul. "Blessed are the poor" means that the poor are close to God and, thus, significant and worthy of respect. All this expresses the values of Informal people.

In the theory of 16 basic desires, humility is an expression of a weak desire for status. Religious teachings encourage humility and recognize excessive pride as sinful. Further, vows of poverty in asceticism and monasticism express the values of Informal people. Members of religious orders dress plainly and simply.

Historically, church leaders have supported the social order and, thus, the wealthy or upper class. The doctrine of the "divine right of kings" is a case in point. In this doctrine both state and church unite to recognize the king as the human being with greatest status, which is second only to God. This doctrine supports the values of Formal people.

Churches vary in how hierarchical they are. In some religions, the higher up you are in the church hierarchy, the closer you are to God, and the greater is your status. In the Roman Catholic hierarchy, for example, the Pope sits at the top of the hierarchy, followed by the cardinals, archbishops, bishops, and priests. Formal people are likely to be attentive to church hierarchical distinctions. On the other hand, Judaism does not have a Pope or well-defined hierarchy as does Catholicism.

The Hindu caste system recognizes four groups varying in status: the Brahmins, or seers, who include intellectuals, artists, and priests; the kshatriyas, who are born administrators; the vaishyas, who make things; and the shudras, who are unskilled laborers or servants. A person's caste has implications for the class of people the individual should associate with.

Siddhartha Gautama, who founded Buddhism, placed relatively little value on status. He preached a religion with no priestly class. He quit the language of Sanskrit and embraced the vernacular of people of faith. Surface distinctions of class and caste meant so little to him that he often appears not even to have noticed them (Smith, 1991, p. 89).

Expensive, famous churches have a high degree of status, while inexpensive, plain churches have average status or less depending on their prestige. The National Cathedral in Washington, D.C., St. Peter's Basilica in Rome, and the Salt Lake Temple of the Church of Jesus Christ of Latter-day Saints are all high-status places of worship because of their fame and expense. Many well-to-do suburban areas in America have expensive churches, temples, and synagogues.

Sometimes status is expressed in subtle ways. A good case in point is the distinction between heaven and hell, which was discussed previously as relevant to the basic desire for acceptance. Here I just want to comment on why heaven is "up there," while hell is "down there." It is primal for humans to think of tall as having a higher status than short, so that "up there" has a higher status than "down there."

In summary, the basic desire for status motivates people to value social standing. Formal people have a strong need for status, while Informal people have a weak need. To help the faithful balance their experiences of status to the psychological level most meaningful to them, religions offer a number of beliefs and practices—notably the concept of divinity, caste system, church hierarchy, and expensive cathedrals—that validate the importance of status. Religions also offer other beliefs and practices—notably God blessing the poor, encouragement of humility, and vows of poverty—that diminish the importance of status. Each person of faith can pick and choose from among these religious phenomena in order to manage his or her experience of status to a valued level, which varies depending on who we are. When a person of faith feels insignificant, the individual may be comforted believing God is watching. Nobody created by (or observed by) God could possibly be insignificant. When a person of faith feels excessively prideful, the individual can consider how unimpressed God is with his or her social standing or wealth.

THE STRIVING FOR SAFETY

The basic desire for tranquility motivates people to do what they can to avoid or minimize experiencing anxiety and pain. In the early 1980s my colleagues and I predicted and then discovered anxiety sensitivity (Reiss, Peterson, Gursky, & McNally, 1986), or the idea that everyone isn't equally motivated to avoid anxiety and pain. Validated in more than 2,000 scientific studies, the construct

Table 7-15
Religion and Tranquility

REDUCES FEAR	INCREASES FEAR
Afterlife, Immortality of Soul	Devil, Occult
Divine Oversight/ Protection	Fires of Hell
Meditation	Judgment
Ritual	Fire, Brimstone,and Magic
Faith Healing	

of anxiety sensitivity is at the forefront of efforts to study the psychology of Post-traumatic Stress Disorder, Panic Disorder, and other anxiety disorders. It implies that Cautious people, who have a strong need for tranquility, tolerate little anxiety and pain and, thus, are highly motivated to avoid these experiences. They tend to have many fears and may like to stay close to home where they feel safe. Cautious people may be timid and possibly anxious. In contrast, Adventurous people, who have a weak need for tranquility, tolerate moderate levels of anxiety and pain and even may seek out danger for its inherent thrills. They tend to have few fears and may like to travel.

Table 7-15 presents some of the religious beliefs and practices that address the basic desire for tranquility.

Some religious phenomena reduce anxiety and fear and, thus, address the needs of Cautious people. Foremost among these is the religious concept of an afterlife. Everybody has wondered what happens to us when we die. Does death bring nothingness or does the soul somehow continue on. Perhaps because we sometimes have dreams in which deceased people appear, beliefs in an afterlife are very common. According to the results of the 1999 General Social Survey, 80 percent of Christians and about 40 percent of Jews, believe in an afterlife. Similar results have been reported by Gallup polls. Every time we imagine talking with a deceased spouse or parent, we are acting as if we believe in an afterlife. Senator Ted Kennedy's son, for example, left a message at his father's gravesite regarding the passage of national health insurance legislation. The message read, "The unfinished business is done."

The faithful conceive of God as a father figure who looks over them and stands ready to protect them from harm. This belief reduces the fear of harm. When the crops are devastated by droughts or some other calamity, believers have faith that God will provide the food they need to survive. Some believe that heavenly angels protect them. The results of surveys have shown that people think of angels as likeable, friendly, benign, and helpful.

Meditation is a common religious method for experiencing tranquility. By practicing muscle relaxation, controlled breathing, and by focusing one's thoughts on religious or peaceful matters, we can learn to relax. This reduces anxiety and fear.

We have previously considered religious rituals as a method for experiencing order. But religious rituals also reduce anxiety. This is partially because rituals create familiarity, which reduces the fear of the unknown. We practice rituals over and over again and the familiarity has a reassuring aspect to it.

Religious faith can reduce the fear of illness. In his 1999 book *The Healing Power of Faith*, physician Harold G. Koenig tells of a number of patients he treated whose faith kept them calm in the face of chronic illness, painful surgeries, and medical adversity. One such woman, Edna, was 75 years old and faced a second hip replacement because her first one did not graft. When asked how she was coping, she said she was angry at first, and then depressed, but when she turned to reading scripture and saying the Lord's Prayer out loud, she became calm. "The Bible just brings comfort," she says page [p 19].

The clergy play an important role in comforting people facing adversity. Even when the clergy are helpless to cure a cancer or support the family member of an alcoholic, simply listening and providing support can go a long way in helping people find meaning in their suffering.

Other religious phenomena increase anxiety and fear, and thus, may address the needs of Adventurous people. We already considered how religious teachings about divine judgment could significantly increase the fear of death. The Egyptians warned that if judged unfavorably after death, wicked pharaohs could be thrown into a snake pit. Christians warn that the wicked will burn forever in the fires of hell. These teachings add the fear of pain to the fear of death.

The primal reaction to the unknown is fear mixed with attraction. By presenting the divine as a mysterious being, religions increase the fear of the unknown. In religious awe the faithful fear the God they believe protects them. The Bible says,

> And his delight shall be the fear of the Lord (Isaiah 11:3).
>
> For as high as the heavens are above earth, so great is his steadfast love toward those who fear him (Psalms 103:11).
>
> The fear of the Lord is the beginning of knowledge... (Proverbs 1:7).
>
> Honor everyone. Love the brotherhood. Fear God. Honor the emperor (1 Peter 2:17).

In his book *The Idea of Holy*, Rudolf Otto (1936) analyzed the fear of God as dread of an unknowable, mysterious reality much greater than ourselves. He regarded the fear of God as a *positive* spiritual experience. He expressed an *attraction* to God based on this fear. Otto's fear of God is a fear of the unknown combined with awe of God's magnificence. He wrote,

> God is a 'mysterium tremendum' [tremendous mystery]. He is not only unknown, but also unknowable. Since he is ineffable and beyond description, we have no words to describe him; all we can do is say what he is not." (Otto, 1936).

Whereas beliefs in God as a protective father-figure reduce our anxiety, belief in the devil increases anxiety. Typically the devil is presented as an entity who opposes the divine and who takes delight in human suffering. He arranges for injurious accidents, premature deaths, and intense pain.

Some priests and ministers give sermons, known as "fire and brimstone," which are intended to scare the congregation into obedience to God. In primitive society shamans use magic to scare tribal members and convince them of the shaman's close relationship with sacred power. Priests who try to build their congregation by scaring people to embrace God may find instead that they have scared people away from religion. Nevertheless, some Adventurous people may be attracted to fire and brimstone for the thrills.

In summary, the basic desire for tranquility motivates people to manage anxiety and fear. Cautious people have relatively little tolerance and place above-average value on safety. Adventurous people have relatively high tolerance and may value dare or risk. To help the faithful manage their experiences of anxiety and fear to the psychological level most meaningful to them, religion offers a number of beliefs and practices—notably the conception of God as protector, the ideas of immortality of the soul and afterlife —that reduce anxiety and fear. Religion also offers other beliefs and practices—notably the conception of a devil, afterlife punishment for wickedness, and the mysterious nature of the divine—that enhance or increase anxiety and fear. Each person of faith can combine these religious phenomena to manage his or her anxieties to a desired level, which varies depending on who we are. When a person of faith feels anxious, he or she can seek comfort in divine protection. When a person of faith is relaxed to the point of boredom, he or she can contemplate Judgment and the possibility of being condemned to the fires of hell.

THE STRIVING FOR REVENGE

People vary in their inclination to confront those who have offended, insulted, or taken advantage of them. Warriors, who have a strong basic desire, typically are quick to confront people they feel are threats to them or their loved ones. They may be pugnacious, aggressive, combative, and perhaps quick to anger. Peace- makers, who have a weak basic desire, typically avoid confrontations even when provoked. They may be kind, forgiving, and gentle. Warriors

Table 7-16

Religion and Revenge

EXPRESSES WARRIOR VALUES	EXPRESSES PEACEMAKER VALUES
Gods of Battles	Forgiving
God's Wrath	"Turn Other Cheek"
Holy Wars/Intolerance	Nonviolence
"Tooth for Tooth"	

typically find meaning in victory and conquest, while Peacemakers typically find meaning in cooperation and conflict avoidance.

Table 7-16 shows some of the religious phenomena that address the basic desire for vengeance. Consistent with the theory of 16 strivings for God, some of these beliefs and practices express the values of Warriors, while others express the values of Peacekeepers.

Religions express the values of Warriors when they encourage worshipping gods of war. The ancient Egyptians and Greeks, for example, each recognized about a dozen or so "war gods." Yahweh, the Hebrew God, originated as a tribal god of war (Armstrong, 1993, p. 50). The Judeo-Christian deity is a god of peace, but this does not prevent some believers from praying to him for victories in war.

The wrath of God inspires people with a Warrior personality type. The prophets of the Old Testament feared God's awful wrath:

> *"And I will strike down upon thee with great vengeance and furious anger at those who attempt to poison and destroy my brothers. And you will know my name is the Lord when I lay my vengeance upon thee" (Ezekiel 25:17).*

The wrath of God can inspire Warriors to imitate him and exact revenge on their enemies.

Although the Old Testament focuses more on the wrath of God than the New Testament does, history offers many examples of Christians citing religion to justify violence or wars. The Crusades were Christian military adventures against Muslims who held territory in the Holy Land. In 1095 Pope Urban II declared the war against the Muslims a "holy war." The Wars of Religion in sixteenth-century France were fought between the Huguenots (Protestants) and the Roman Catholics. To this day, religious intolerance is a potentially significant instigator of violence, as we see in some examples of hatred between Muslims and Christian fundamentalists.

Islam offers the concept of a holy war called jihad. It teaches Muslims to defend themselves against their enemies, but not to attack first because God hates the aggressor.

The Old Testament says that a person who injures another should provide equal retribution to the injured party. This idea of an "eye for an eye" imbues the concept of just revenge with religious significance:

> If men strike, and hurt a woman with child, so that her fruit depart from her, and yet no mischief follow: he shall surely be punished, according as the woman's husband will lay upon him; and he shall pay as the judges determine. And if any mischief follows, then thou shalt give life for life, i.e. eye for eye, tooth for tooth, hand for hand, foot for foot; burning for burning, wound for wound, stripe for stripe (Exodus 21: 22-25).

Some scholars say the message of an "eye for an eye" was not to encourage vengeance but to restrict it to the value of the damage. In other words, if somebody causes you to lose your hand, you can take the person's hand, but you can't go further and kill the individual. Speaking as a psychologist, however, I think such subtleties may be lost on many ordinary people, who I suspect interpret an "eye for an eye" as justification for vengeance even if that was not the true religious intent or meaning.

On the other hand, some religious phenomena contradict the values of Warriors and instead express the values of Peacemakers. In his "Sermon on the Mount," Jesus says:

You have heard that it was said, "An eye for an eye, and a tooth for a tooth." But I tell you, do not resist an evil person. If someone strikes you on the right cheek, turn to him the other also. And if someone wants to sue you and take your tunic, let him have your cloak as well. If someone forces you to go one mile, go with him two miles. Give to the one who asks you, and do not turn away from the one who wants to borrow from you (Matthew 5:38–42).

The Old Testament says:

"And the Lord spoke to Moses, saying: 'Thou shalt not hate thy brother in thine heart; thou shalt not in any wise rebuke thy neighbor, and not suffer sin upon him. Thou shalt not avenge, nor bear any grudge against the children of thy people, but thou shalt love thy neighbor as thyself: I am the Lord'" (Leviticus 19:17–18).

The prophets taught that God is merciful: "For the Lord God is a merciful God" (Deuteronomy 4:31). God's compassion and mercy are cited frequently in the Koran. The conception of a merciful God inspires the faithful to imitate him and to let provocations go by without seeking revenge. It imbues the values of Peacemakers with divine significance.

The following passage of the Bible limits and reduces vengeance, violence, and aggression. Ordinary people interpret it to mean they should resist anger and try to let provocations go by. In short, the passage offers inspiration for Peacemakers.

The Bible says:

All nations shall beat their swords into ploughshares, and their spears into pruninghooks: nation shall not lift up sword against nation, neither shall they learn war anymore (Isaiah 2:4).

Many clergy teach the faithful to love thy neighbor; that anger is blind; and that hatred is evil.

The Buddha's sermons condemned violence. The Dalai Lama, who has been criticized for being a pacifist, claimed there has never been a "Buddhist war." The Buddha taught that wisdom and compassion are two qualities essential for realizing enlightenment.

In summary, the basic desire for vengeance motivates people to manage confrontation, conflict, and aggression. To help the faithful manage their experiences of confrontation to the psychological level most meaningful to them, religion offers a number of beliefs and practices—notably the wrath of God, the concept of holy war, and the philosophy of an "eye for an eye"—that increase, encourage, or sanction vengeance. It also offers other beliefs and practices—notably the philosophy of "turn the other cheek" and Buddhist compassion—that express the values of Peacemakers. Each person of faith can combine these religious phenomena to manage his or her vengeance to a desired level, which varies depending on who the individual is. When a person of faith feels angry, he or she can turn the other cheek to reduce vengeance. When a person of faith is having difficulty standing up to an aggressor, he or she can reflect on God's wrath to arouse the fighting spirit.

8

CONCLUSION

We go through life seeking to satisfy the 16 basic desires that move us. Basic desires can be satisfied only temporarily, never permanently. Soon after we satisfy a basic desire, it recurs to motivate us anew. We experience hunger, we eat, and hours later we again become hungry. We experience loneliness, we socialize, and a day or two later we again feel lonely. We experience outrage at some injustice, we help the victim, and days or weeks later we experience outrage pertaining to some other injustice. Since we need to satisfy the same basic desires over and over again, we embrace beliefs and behaviors that help us do this.

We are particularly motivated to satisfy both our strong basic desires and our weak basic desires. Which of the 16 basic desires are strong or weak depends on our values, and they usually change little from about age 30 to about 55 (Reiss & Havercamp, 1975). Your strongest desire might be to spend time with your family, but your spouse's strongest desire might be for career success.

Here is my theory in a sentence: People embrace religion because it provides them with opportunities to satisfy their basic desires again and again. It offers repeated opportunities to satisfy all 16 basic desires. It addresses each of the 16 basic desires both in strong form and in weak form. In theory each major religion does this although here we examined primarily the Judeo-Christian religions. I hope future scholars examine in more detail how the 16 basic desires play out in other world religions.

According to Pals (2006), scholars have published about eight comprehensive theories on the essence of religious experiences. We briefly considered these theories in Chapter 1. Each theory is fascinating but not widely accepted as valid. In my opinion, each theory explains religious experiences in terms of just one or two basic desires when religion addresses 16 basic desires.

Previous scholars including Freud, James, Durkheim, Fraser, Niebuhr, and Rashdall did not successfully identify the essence of religion as the fear of death, mysticism, sacredness, magic, transcendence, or morality because religion has no single essence. Religion is about the values motivated by the 16 basic desires of human nature. It has mass appeal because it accommodates the values of people with opposite personality traits. No matter what your personality type—Warrior or Peacemaker, Introvert or Extrovert, Idealist or Realist, Assertive or Onlooker—religion offers some beliefs and practices that express your values.

The ideas advanced in this book are part of a new, comprehensive psychological theory of religious experiences called the "16 strivings for God." The theory is new primarily because it expresses original ideas about human motivation, desires, and values. Virtually every psychologist defines motivation as psychic energy or drive; I define motivation as the assertion of core values. We are a species motivated to assert our values. The way to motivate someone is to appeal to his or her values.

This is the first new comprehensive psychological theory of religious experiences since Freud and James published their ideas more than a century ago. Maslow (1994/1964) published important psychological analyses of religious experiences, but he concentrated on the study of peak experiences and did not examine a comprehensive range of religious experiences. Some positive psychologists have put forth interesting ideas about religion and happiness (Seligman, 2011), but they have yet to pull together these ideas into a comprehensive theory with many specific predictions.

The theory of 16 strivings for God can be scientifically evaluated. Future researchers can use conventional research methods in psychology to determine which of the many predictions in this book are valid and which are invalid. In contrast, Freud offered ideas about religion that cannot be studied scientifically.

EVIDENCE

In the balance of this chapter, I will summarize the evidence relevant to my theory of religion. As a scientific theory, each piece of evidence is open to challenge, debate, and future research. Each is open to critical analysis regarding the quality of the evidence. Each requires additional research and study before firm conclusions can be drawn. What can be said now with a high degree of confidence is that the 16 basic desires play out in religious experience.

SPIRITUAL PERSONALITY

One of the strengths of my theory of 16 strivings is that it potentially describes our individual spiritual needs in greater detail, and with greater validity, as compared to the alternative theories of religion discussed in Chapter 1. In 1902 William James observed that we are individuals in terms of our spiritual needs. He wrote,

> The divine can mean no single quality, it must mean a group of qualities, by being champions of which in alternation, different men may all find worthy missions. Each attitude being a syllable in human nature's total message, it takes the whole of us to spell the meaning out completely. So a god of battles must be allowed to be the god for one kind of person, a god of peace and heaven and home, the god for another.... If we are peevish and jealous, destruction of the self must be an element of our religion; why need it be one if we are good and sympathetic from the outset?

> If we are sick souls, we require a religion of deliverance; but why think so much of deliverance, if we are healthy minded. (p. 420)

Although James's analysis is insightful, it is lacking in detail. He did not say what spiritual experiences most people need. He did not delineate, for example, the spiritual needs of Intellectuals versus Practical people, or of Idealists versus Realists. He did not know about the 16 basic desires. His list of needs, which he called instincts, was incomplete. Without details connecting personality and spirituality, psychologists did not know how to explore scientifically the validity of James's insight. They admired James's ideas, but they did not have scientific methods to study them.

Our theory of 16 strivings fills in many of the details omitted from James's analysis of individuality and spirituality. How a person prioritizes the 16 basic desires seems to correspond to those aspects of religion that resonate with the person. As was discussed in Chapter 3, for example, Emma has a strong basic desire for family and embraces religion to support her family values. Tom is an intellectual who finds meaning in understanding life from a religious perspective. Both are religious people, but for different psychological reasons. We need additional research on the correspondence between an individual's desire profile and his or her interest in various aspects of religion.

DIVINE ATTRIBUTES

The theory of 16 strivings for God potentially explains how human beings conceive of the divine. In our scientific surveys that led to the delineation of 16 basic desires, we did not ask a single question about religion, God, or spirituality. Later, when we were asked how the 16 basic desires relate to religion, we had no particular expectation of what we might learn. We were stunned to discover that the greatest imaginable expressions of 13 basic desires are attributes of the Judeo-Christian conception of God. (See Table 8-1.) The basic desires for eating and romance are not connected to divine attributes because the Judeo-Christian God has no body, does not eat, and is not a romantic figure.

Table 8-1
God's Attributes as Expressions of Basic Desires

BASIC DESIRE	DIVINE ATTRIBUTION
Acceptance	Salvation
Curiosity	Omniscience
Eating	
Family	God as Son
Honor	God as Father, Moral Lawgiver
Idealism	Just
Independence	Self-Sufficient
Order	Immortal, Eternal Nature of God
Physical Activity	Almighty
Power	Lord, Creator
Romance	
Saving	
Social Contact	God as Friend
Status	Divinity
Tranquility	Protector
Vengeance	Wrath of God

Other major religions also conceive of divinity in ways that express basic desires. In the Hindu Trimurti (trinity), for example, Brahma is creator, which is an expression of the basic desire for power; Vishnu is preserver and protector, which are expressions of the basic desires for order, tranquility, and honor; and Shiva is the god of destruction, which is an expression of the basic desire for vengeance. Since Hindu deities have sex, eat, and drink, they express basic desires not expressed by the Judeo-Christian conception of God.

Compared to our thesis of 16 strivings for God, some of the alternative theories of religion appear to be less powerful in explaining human images of the divine. Freud's insight on imagining God as a protective father figure seems compelling, but theories that posit a "single essence" for religion, such as transcendence, mysticism, or morality, do not explain well why humans conceive of God as having multiple attributes such as omniscience, omnipotence, logos, and compassion.

Our thesis creates new opportunities to study the possible connections between basic desires and divine attributes. Are desire profiles correlated with interest in different divine attributes? Do different basic desires motivate the various images of divinity associated with different religions? From a scientific perspective the results of such studies could expand our knowledge of religious experiences.

ASCETICISM

My theory suggests new ideas for studying asceticism. The practice of asceticism has long been associated with religion and the spiritual life. It is particularly challenging to explain because psychologists typically assume that people seek pleasure and reject pain, but ascetics do the opposite. Freudian psychologists speculated that ascetics are guilt-ridden and feel unworthy of pleasure. In Chapter 5 we considered the possibility that asceticism is motivated by the positive affirmation of certain values. Specifically, I suggested that ascetic practices may satisfy these basic desires: a strong need for honor combined with weak needs for eating, status, social contact, family, and tranquility.

Future research is needed to evaluate the extent to which the suggested profile provides a valid explanation for asceticism. Researchers might learn that the profile is valid, partially valid, or invalid. They might modify or strengthen the suggested profile based on the results of their studies.

MYSTICISM

The origins of the world's major religions can be traced to the mystical experiences of the founders. Although some scholars have sought to explain mysticism as a drug-induced altered state of consciousness, in Chapter 6 we learned that certain basic desires might be particularly relevant to motivating mystical experiences. A very weak basic desire for vengeance motivates people to value and to find meaning in harmony, which is a prominent feature of mystical experiences. A very weak basic desire for independence motivates people to value interconnectedness or unity, which is another prominent feature of mysticism. People with weak basic desires for both vengeance and independence should be much more likely to have mystical experiences, as compared to those who have average or strong basic desires for both vengeance and independence. Mysticism also may be associated with weak basic desires for intellectual curiosity and power as well as with an average need for romance.

These comments show how the theory of 16 strivings for God offers new ideas and research opportunities regarding the psychology of mysticism. Future research is needed to evaluate the correspondence between the suggested desire profile for mysticism and actual mystical experiences.

RELIGIOUS BELIEFS AND PRACTICES

The 16 strivings for God may help us understand the psychological basis for numerous religious beliefs and practices. In theory, nearly every religious story, symbol, or experience—such as Creation, the Ten Commandments, and the Sermon on the Mount—expresses one or more of the values motivated by the 16 basic desires.

As shown in Table 8-2, all 16 basic desires are connected to religious phenomena. In many instances these connections are obvious after they are briefly explained. From a psychological standpoint, for example, Creation is the greatest imaginable achievement and, thus, is an expression of the basic desire for power. Rituals express the basic desire for order because they structure our lives. Religious celebrations typically involve dancing, which is an expression of the basic desire for physical activity combined with the basic desire for romance. Church activities include charitable giving and efforts to strengthen the community, which are expressions of the basic desire for idealism.

Theoretically, each of the world's major religions expresses all 16 basic desires. Yet any particular religion might address some basic desires more comprehensively than others. As shown in

Table 8-2

Religious Beliefs and Practices as Expressions of Basic Desires

BASIC DESIRE	RELIGIOUS BELIEF OR PRACTICE
Acceptance	Salvation, Forgiveness, Baptism, Positive Thinking
Curiosity	Omniscience, Logos, Theology
Eating	Eucharist, Dietary Laws, Feasts
Family	God as Father, Church Events
Honor	Moral Rules, Self-Discipline, Penitence, Ethnic Loyalty
Idealism	Social Gospel, Charity
Independence	Free Will, God as Self-Sufficient
Order	Rituals, Divine Order, Eternal Nature of God, Cleanliness
Physical Activity	Church Programs, God as Almighty, Dancing
Power	Creation, Omnipotent, Lord, Miracles, Magic
Romance	Holy Matrimony, Sexual Imagery, Fertility Rites, Dancing
Saving	Religious Relics, Bible Stories
Social Contact	God as Friend, Angels, Fellowship, Festivals
Status	Divinity, Divine Right of Kings, Caste System
Tranquility	Afterlife, Divine Protection, Faith Healing, Meditation
Vengeance	Wrath of God, Religious Wars, Intolerance

Table 8-2, the Judeo-Christian religions provide multiple phenomena expressing the basic desires for acceptance, honor, order, and tranquility. They provide fewer phenomena, and thus may give less emphasis, to the basic desires for eating, physical activity, romance, and saving.

In conclusion, it is not just one or two aspects of religion that express basic desires. It is not just one or two basic desires that play

Table 8-3

Religious Opposites with Respect to Basic Desires

BASIC DESIRE	EXPRESSION	OPPOSITE
Acceptance	Salvation, Forgiveness	Damnation
Curiosity	Logos	Revelation
Eating	Feasts	Fasting
Family	God as Son	God Before Family
Honor	Morality	Sin
Idealism	Charity	Tolerates Evil
Independence	Free Will	Mystical Union, Gratitude
Order	Rituals	Chaos
Physical Activity	Church Fitness Programs	Sabbath
Power	Lord	Submission
Romance	Holy Matrimony	Celibacy
Saving	Religious Relics	
Social Contact	Fellowship	Solitude
Status	Divinity	Humility
Tranquility	Afterlife	Fearing God
Vengeance	Wrath of God	Turn Other Cheek

out in religion. Virtually all aspects of religion are expressions of basic desires.

CONTRADICTIONS OF HUMAN NATURE

As predicted by my theory of 16 basic desires, religions offer beliefs and practices that express strong versions of each basic desire, and they offer beliefs and practices that express weak versions of each basic desire. As shown in Table 8-3, religious beliefs and practices are in opposites with respect to each basic desire.

Many of the apparent contradictions in religion are not arbitrary errors in theology. They arise because of human individuality, and they correspond closely to the contradictions of human nature. Religion contradicts itself at times because it addresses the needs of people with diverse personality traits, which come in opposites (e.g., introvert-extrovert, intellectual-practical, timid-adventurous).

The theory of 16 strivings for God may be the only psychological theory that potentially explains why religions embrace opposite values, as in the examples of praying to a God of peace for victory in war, or fearing the God who keeps us safe. Since all human motives manifest in both strong and weak versions, all core values come in opposites, most personality traits come in opposites, and many religious practices and beliefs come in psychological opposites.

COMPARATIVE RELIGION: DO DIFFERENT DENOMINATIONS SATISFY DIFFERENT DESIRES?

My thesis offers many opportunities to compare typical desire profiles associated with interest in various religions. Although all major religions address the 16 basic desires, they may differ in how comprehensively or effectively they address certain desires. They may differ with regard to how strongly they embrace specific core values. Catholicism, for example, might be particularly effective in addressing the need for family. Catholic doctrine holds that human beings were created to be family-oriented people. The Trinity is a model of life-giving love within the family unit. Pope John Paul II's apostolic exhortation titled, "On the Role of the Christian Family in the Modern World," states that marriage and family constitute one of the most precious of human values.

Buddhism may be less consistently positive about family life as compared to Christianity. The Buddha taught that family attachments could be obstacles on the path toward enlightenment. He himself left behind his family when he set out to live in the wilderness for the purpose of seeking enlightenment. These aspects of Buddhism might resonate with what I call in Chapter 7 the "Adult-Focused" personality. In theory, these are individuals born with a weaker-than-average parenting instinct.

Both Catholicism and Buddhism embrace the basic desire for family, but they may value it differently. As compared with Buddhism, Catholicism might be more consistent in placing high value on family life.

Christianity and Hinduism may value differently the basic desire for status. In Matthew 5:3 the Christian Bible blesses the poor in spirit and states they will inherit Heaven. Humility is regarded as a virtue and pride as a sin.

Hinduism imbues status with spiritual significance. The Hindu caste system is a salient aspect of that religion. Hinduism maintains strict rules about caste and talks a lot about what caste means in terms of everyday life. Does this suggest that Hinduism places a higher value on satisfying the basic desire for status than does Catholicism?

Hinduism may value individuality more than does Catholicism. It recognizes four different paths for spiritual fulfillment: The Way to God through Knowledge; the Way through Love; the Way through Work; and the Way through Psychophysical Exercise. Each individual may choose the path that is best for him or her. Both individuality and choice (self-determination) fall under the basic desire for independence. In contrast, Catholicism presents the faithful with the conception of a personal God who is to be obeyed. It places less emphasis on individual differences in how best to seek God or practice the faith.

Buddhism presents a conception of enlightenment as nirvana, or a state free from the burdens, discomforts, and pain of finite existence. Does this mean that Buddhism may satisfy the basic desire for tranquility more effectively than do other religions? According to the theory of 16 basic desires, people with a high need for tranquility place a much higher value on minimizing anxiety and pain than do people with a low need for tranquility.

Future researchers might assess the composite desire profiles by asking representative groups from various religions to complete the RMP questionnaire to learn what it is about religion that people find most satisfying. Researchers might evaluate, for example, whether Hindus who have a high need for status express greater satisfaction with their religion than do Buddhists who have a high need for status. Do Catholics who have a high need for family express greater satisfaction with their religion than do Catholics who have a low need for family? Researchers might study scores of similar questions that arise from considering various religions and denominations from the perspective of the 16 basic desires.

PSYCHOLOGICAL SCIENCE AND RELIGIOUS EXPERIENCE

Good scientific theories articulate new issues for future research and suggest the methods needed to study those issues. They put forth interesting ideas to attract new researchers into a field, in this case the psychology of religion. They are born out of curiosity and give rise to more questions than they answer. They offer exciting new insights and facts, but not absolute truths. In science, it is only a matter of time before so-called truths are replaced by deeper truths learned by a new generation of researchers.

To be successful this book does not need to offer absolute truths. God gives absolute truths; psychologists just give theories. Science is an endless process of discovery. Although my taxonomy of human needs is superior to the lists of needs generated at Harvard during the period of 1890-1970, in due course some future researcher will produce a much better taxonomy.

The ideas put forth in this book may have significant implications for pastoral counseling and faith-based therapy. When a person is having trouble in a relationship, at work, at school, or even in athletics, Reiss Profile® Masters who are trained to apply my theory to life coaching ask, "What basic desires are frustrated in the individual's life? What is the conflict of values between the person and the work or home situation?" I think my theory of religion is potentially applicable to pastoral counseling and faith-based therapy although pastoral counseling is beyond the scope of this book.

William James's work on religious experience was exceptional. He described the extraordinary variety of religious experiences. He understood that spirituality is a plural construct. Religion is at its best when its message is inclusiveness. As James put it, we cannot spell out the full meaning of spirituality unless we study everyone.

James suggested that some people need a god of battles, but those with troubled souls need a savior. In Chapter 3 we learned that Emma needs a god with family values, but Tom needs an omniscient god. Look at the 16 basic desires in strong and in weak form. What god do you need?

ACKNOWLEDGMENTS

The author wrote seven drafts of this book between the years 2008 and 2015. The author would like to recognize the generous assistance and encouragement of these individuals:

Frederick Andrie

Ralph W. Hood, Jr., Ph.D.

Andrew McKinnon, Ph.D.

Mary-Ellen Milos, Ph.D.

James T. Napolitan, Ph.D.

Maggi M. Reiss, M.A.

C. Renee Yarmuth, D.Min.

ABOUT THE AUTHOR

Steven Reiss is a retired tenured Professor of Psychology at The Ohio State University. He was born in New York City in 1947 and was educated at Dartmouth College (A.B.), Yale University (Ph.D.), and Harvard Medical School (clinical psychology internship). In 1971 he married Maggi Musico. Maggi and Steven have two adult children and a grandchild.

Reiss led the research team that discovered anxiety sensitivity. In the 1990s anxiety sensitivity became one of the most widely studied and important topics in clinical psychology. Anxiety sensitivity changed how therapists evaluate and treat Panic Disorder and Posttraumatic Stress Disorder.

In the 1980s and 1990s Reiss was a nationally active member of the generation of scientists, therapists, and advocates who worked to integrate people with intellectual disabilities into community settings. Community supports were created, and custodial-care institutions closed. This movement significantly changed the lives of millions of people over a period of about thirty years. The life of a child born today with intellectual disabilities will be very different from the lives of those born during the 1970s.

In the 1980s Reiss became a leading scientific authority on "dual diagnosis" or the co-occurrence of mental illness and intellectual disabilities. In 1980 Reiss founded an outpatient clinic for dual diagnosis serving the Chicago metropolitan area. This was one of the first outpatient programs for dual diagnosis in the nation. Reiss introduced the now widely-used term "diagnostic overshadowing" to refer to the tendency to overlook the mental health needs of people with developmental disabilities. In 1987 he organized the first-ever international conference on the mental health aspects of intellectual disabilities. The Director of the National Institute of Mental Health convened an ad hoc panel to fast track funding for Reiss's conference. Also in 1987 he published the *Reiss Screen for Maladaptive Behavior*, which became the leading method in North America for screening for dual diagnosis. Reiss's work on intellectual disabilities was recognized with four national awards including the 2008 Distinguished Research Award from the American Association on Intellectual and Developmental Disabilities (AAIDD), the 2006 Frank J. Menolascino Award for Career Research from the National Association on Dual Diagnosis, the 1991 Distinguished Award for Career Research from the Arc of the United States, and the 1987 Distinguished Services Award from AAIDD.

Reiss and his colleagues executed the first large scale, scientific research surveys of what people say motivates them. The results identified 16 psychological needs or "basic desires," which are goals common to everyone and deeply rooted in human nature. Reiss applied the 16 basic desires to new methods of life coaching, education, relationships, and religion.

RELATED BOOKS BY STEVEN REISS

Who Am I: The 16 Basic Desires That Motivate Our Actions and Define Our Personalities. New York: Jeremy B. Tarcher/Putnam, 2000.

The Normal Personality: A New Way of Thinking about People. New York: Cambridge University Press, 2008.

Myths of Intrinsic Motivation. Columbus, OH: IDS Publishing, 2013.

REFERENCES

Abhayuananda, S. (1996). *History of Mysticism: The Unchanging Testament.* London: Alma Books.

Adler, A. (1964/1927). *The Practice and Theory of Individual Psychology.* New York: Harcourt Brace Jovanovich.

Alexander, F. (2001/1932). *The Use of the Self.* New York: E. P. Orion Publishing.

Allport, G. W. (1961). *The Individual and His Religion.* New York: Macmillan.

Angels, K. L., Woodward, A., & Underwood, A. (2010). Sociology of religion. In S. C. Monahan, W. A. Mirola, and M. A. O. Emerson (Eds.), *Sociology of Religion Reader* (2nd edition). New York: Pearson.

Aquinas, T. (1961/1259). *On the Truth of the Catholic Faith.* New York: Doubleday.

Aristotle (1953/330 B.C.E.). *The Nichomachean Ethics* (translated by J. A. K. Thompson). New York: Penquin Books. (Original work created about 330 B.C.E.).

Armstrong, K. (2009). *The Case for God.* New York: Alfred A. Knopf.

Armstrong, K. (1993). *A History of God.* New York: Ballantine Books.

Augustine, S. (1964/397). Confessions (translated by A. C. Outler). In J. H. Hick (Ed.), *Classical and Contemporary Readings in the Philosophy of Religion* (pp. 19-28). Philadelphia: The Westminister Press.

Bell, C. (2000). *Ritual: Perspectives and Dimensions.* Oxford, England: Oxford University Press.

Borchert, B. (1994). *Mysticism: Its History and Challenge.* Newburyport, MA: Red Wheel/Weiser.

Darwin, C. (1965). *The Expression of the Emotions in Man and Animals.* Chicago: The University of Chicago Press. (Original work published in 1872).

Darwin, C. (1859). *The Origin of the Species.* London: Murray.

Deci, E. L., Koestner, R., & Ryan, R. M. (1999). A meta-analytic review of experiments examining the effects of extrinsic rewards on intrinsic motivation. *Psychological Bulletin, 125,* 627-668.

Dunlap, K. (1919). Are there any instincts? *Journal of Abnormal Psychology, 14,* 307-311.

Durkheim, E. (1965/1915). *Elementary Forms of the Religious Life* (translated by C. Cosman). New York: Free Press.

Ehrman, B. D. (2010). *Jesus, Interrupted.* New York: HarperOne.

Emmons, R. A. (2007). *THANKS! How the New Science of Gratitude Can Make You Happier.* Boston: Houghton-Mifflin.

Engel, G., Olson, K. R., & Patrick, C. (2002). The personality of love: Fundamental motives and traits related to components of love. *Personality and Individual Differences, 32,* 839-853.

Eron, L. D., & Huesmann, L. R. (1990). The stability of aggressive behavior – even unto the third generation. In M. Lewis and S. M. Miller (Eds.), *Handbook of Developmental Psychology* (pp. 147-156). New York: Plenum.

Feuerbach, L. (1964/1841). Religion as illusion. In J. H. Hick (Ed.), *Classical and Contemporary Readings in the Philosophy of Religion.* Englewood Cliffs, NJ: Prentice-Hall.

Flugel, J. C. (1945). *Man, Morals, and Society.* New York: Viking.

Fontana, D. (2003). *Psychology, Religion, and Spirtuality.* Malden, MA: Blackwell.

Forsyth, J. (2003). *Psychological Theories of Religion.* Upper Saddle, NJ: Prentice-Hall.

Foster, R. J., & Griffin, E. (Eds.) (2000). *Spiritual Classics.* New York: HarperOne.

Frankl, V. E. (2008/1959). *Man's Search for Meaning.* Boston: Beacon.

Franklin, J. (2010). *Fasting.* Lake Mary, FL: Charisma House.

Fraser, J. (2009/1890). *The Golden Bough: A Study in Magic and Religion*. Oxford, England: Oxford University Press.

Freud, S. (1989/1927). *Future of an Illusion*. New York: Norton.

Freud, S. (1963/1916). *Introductory Lectures on Psychoanalysis*. London: Hogarth Press.

Freud, S. (1961/1930). *Civilization and Its Discontents*. New York: Norton.

Freud, S. (1950/1913). *Totem and Taboo*. New York: Norton.

Freud, S. (1939/1967). *Moses and Monotheism*. New York: Vintage Books.

Guzman, G. (2008). Hallucinogenic mushrooms in Mexico: An Overview. *Economic Botany, 62*, 404-412.

Havercamp, S. M., & Reiss, S. (2004). A comprehensive assessment of human striving: Reliability and validity of the Reiss Profile. *Journal of Personality Assessment, 81*, 123-132.

Hick, J. H. (Ed.) (1964). *Classical and Contemporary Readings in the Philosophy of Religion*. Englewood Cliffs, NJ: Prentice-Hall.

Hood, R. W. (1975). The construction and preliminary validation of a measure of reported mystical experience. *Journal for the Scientific Study of Religion, 14 (1)*, 29-41.

Hood, R. W., Hill, P. C., & Spilka, B. (2009). *The Psychology of Religion: An Empirical Approach*. New York: Guilford Press.

Huesmann, L. R., & Eron, L. D. (1988). Individual differences and the trait of aggression. *European Journal of Personality, 3*, 95-106.

Huxley, A. (1953). *The Doors of Perception*. New York: Harper & Brothers.

James, W. (2004/1902). *Varieties of Religious Experience*. New York: Barnes and Noble Books.

James, W. (1918/1890). *The Principles of Psychology (vol. 2)*. New York: Dover.

Jung, C. G. (1960). *The Psychology of Religion*. New Haven, CT: Yale University Press.

Jung, C. G. (1933). *Modern Man in Search of a Soul.* New York: Harcourt.

Jung, C. G. (1923). *Psychological Types.* New York: Harcourt.

Kanfer, F. H., & Phillips, J. S. (1970). *Learning Foundations of Behavior Therapy.* New York: Wiley.

Kant, I. (1998/1781). *Critique of Pure Reason.* New York: Cambridge University Press.

Kempis, T. (2000). Solitude and silence. In R.J. Foster and E. Griffin (Eds.), *Spiritual Classics.* New York: HarperOne.

Kierkegaard, S. (2013/1844). *The Concept of Anxiety.* Princeton, NJ: Princeton University Press.

Kirsch, I. (1990). *Changing Expectations.* Pacific Grove, CA: Brookes-Cole.

Koenig, H. (1999). *The Healing Power of Faith.* New York: Simon & Schuster.

Kroll, J., & Bachrach, B. (2005). *The Mystic Mind: The Psychology of Medieval Mystics and Ascetics.* New York: Routledge.

Lowrie, W. (1968). Kierkegaard's attack upon "Christendom" 1854-1855. *Soren Kierkegaard.* Princeton, NJ: Princeton University Press.

Maslow, A. H. (1994/1964). *Religions, Values, and Peak-Experiences.* New York: Penguin Books.

Maslow, A. H. (1954). *Motivation and Personality.* New York: Harper & Row.

Maslow, A. H. (1943). A theory of motivation. *Psychological Review, 50,* 370-396.

McCann, J. (1958). *Saint Benedict.* Garden City, NY: Image Books.

McClelland, D.C. (1961). *The Achieving Society.* Princeton, NJ: Van Nostrand.

McDougall, W. (2003). *An Introduction to Social Psychology.* Mineola, NY: Dover. (Original work published in 1908).

Menninger, K. (1938). *Man Against Himself.* New York: Harcourt, Brace & World.

Metzner, R. (2004). *Teonanacatl: Sacred Mushroom of Visions*. El Verano, CA: Four Trees Press.

Miller, M. L. (2014). Why are poor people religious? *The humanist.com*, Aug. 27.

Monahan, S. C., Mirola, W. A., & Emerson, M. O. (2010). *Sociology of Religion: A Reader*. London: Pearson.

Murray, H. A. (1943). *Thematic Apperception Test*. Cambridge, MA: Harvard University Press.

Murray, H. A. (1938). *Explorations in Personality: A Clinical and Experimental Study of Fifty Men of College Age*. New York: Oxford University Press.

Niebuhr, E. (1949). *The Nature and Destiny of Man*. New York: Charles Scribner's Sons.

Olson, K. R. (2007). Research on fundamental motives. In L. Brown (Ed.), *Psychology of Motivation* (pp. 1-3). Hauppauge, NY: Nova Science Publishers.

Olson, K. R., & Chapin, B. (2007). Relation of fundamental motives and psychological needs to well being and motivation. In L. Brown (Ed.), *Psychology of Motivation*. Hauppauge, NY: Nova Science Publishers.

Olson, K. R., & Webber, D. (2004). Relations between Big Five traits and fundamental motives. *Psychological Reports, 95*, 795-802.

Otto, R. (1936). *The Idea of Holy*. New York: Oxford University Press.

Paley, W. (2009). *Natural Theology*. Cambridge, England: Cambridge University Press. (Original work published in 1803).

Pals, D. L. (2006). *Eight Theories of Religion*. Oxford, England: Oxford University Press.

Peale, N. V. (1952). *The Power of Positive Thinking*. New York: Ballantine Books.

Pfohl, B. (1996). Obsessiveness. In G. Costello (Ed.), *Personality Characteristics of the Personality Disordered*. New York: Wiley.

Piedmont, R. L. (1999). Does spirituality represent the sixth factor of personality? Spiritual transcendence and the Five-Factor model. *Journal of Personality, 67,* 985-1013.

Piedmont, R. L., Werdekl, M., & Fernando, M. (2009). The Utility of the Assessment of Spirituality and Religious Sentiments (ASPIRES) scale with Christians and Buddhists in Sri Lanka. *Research in the Social Scientific Study of Religion, 20,* 131-143.

Plato (1966). *The Republic of Plato* (translated by F. M. Cornford). New York: Oxford University Press.

Pratt, J. B. (1921). *The Religious Consciousness: A Psychological Study.* New York: Macmillan.

Ramsey, G. (1843). *An Inquiry into the Principle of Human Happiness and Human Duty.* London: William Pickering.

Rashdall, H. (1964/1907). The moral argument for the existence of God. In J. H. Hick (Ed.), *Classical and Contemporary Readings in the Philosophy of Religion* (pp. 268-273). Englewood Cliffs, NJ: Prentice-Hall.

Reiss, S. (2013a). *The Reiss Motivation Profile: What Motivates You?* Columbus, OH: IDS Publishing.

Reiss, S. (2013b). *Myths of Intrinsic Motivation.* Columbus, OH: IDS Publishing.

Reiss, S. (2010). *Human Needs and Intellectual Disabilities: Applications for Person Centered Planning and Crisis Intervention.* Kingston, NY: NADD.

Reiss, S. (2008). *The Normal Personality: A New Way of Thinking about People.* New York: Cambridge University Press.

Reiss, S. (2004a). The 16 strivings for God. *Zygon, 39,* 303-320.

Reiss, S. (2004b). Multifaceted nature of intrinsic motivation: The theory of 16 basic desires. *Review of General Psychology, 8,* 179-193.

Reiss, S. (2000a). *Who Am I? The 16 Basic Desires that Motivate Our Actions and Define Our Personalities.* New York: Tarcher/Putnam.

Reiss, S. (2000b). Why people turn to religion: A motivational analysis. *Journal for the Scientific Study of Religion, 39,* 47-52.

Reiss, S. (1980). Pavlovian conditioning and human fear: An expectancy model. *Behavior Therapy, 11*, 380-396.

Reiss, S., & Havercamp, S.M. (2005). Motivation in developmental context: A new method of studying self-actualization. *Journal of Humanistic Psychology, 45*, 41-53.

Reiss, S., & Havercamp, S.M. (1998). Toward a comprehensive assessment of fundamental motivation. *Psychological Assessment, 10*, 97-106.

Reiss, S., Peterson, R.A., Gursky, D.M., & McNally, R.J. (1986). Anxiety sensitivity, anxiety frequency, and the prediction of fearfulness. *Behavior Research and Therapy, 24*, 1-8.

Russell, B. (1972). *A History of Western Philosophy*. New York: Simon & Schuster. (Original work published in 1945).

Saroglou, V. (2010). Religiousness as a cultural adaptation of basic traits: A Five-Factor model perspective. *Personality and Social Psychology Review, 14*, 109-125.

Saroglou, V. (2008). Individual differences in religion and spirituality: An essay of personality traits and/or values. *Journal for the Scientific Study of Religion, 47*, 83-101.

Seligman, M. E. P. (2011). *Flourish: A Visionary New Understanding of Happiness and Well-Being*. New York: Free Press.

Skinner, B. F. (1938). *The Behavior of Organisms: An Experimental Analysis*. Oxford, England: Appleton-Century.

Smith, H. (1991). *The World's Religions: Our Great Wisdom Traditions*. San Francisco: Harper Collins.

Smith, W. R. (1894). *Lectures on the Religion of the Semites*. London: Adamant Media Corporation.

Stace, W. T. (1960). *Mysticism and Philosophy*. New York: Macmillan.

Tylor, E. B. (1881). *Anthropology: An Introduction to the Study of Man and Civilization*. New York: Appleton and Company.

Vail, K. E., Rothschild, Z. K., Weise, D., Solomon, S., Pyszczynski, T., & Greenberg, J. (2010). A terror management analysis of the psychological functions of religion. *Personality and Social Psychology Review, 14*, 84-94.

Ware, K. (1995). The way of ascetics: Negative or affirmative? In V. L. Wimbush and R. Valantasis (Eds.), *Asceticism* (pp. 3-15). Oxford, England: Oxford University Press.

Wasson, R. G. (1957). Seeking the magic mushroom. *Life Magazine.*

Wasson, R. G., Kramrisch, S., Ott, J., & Ruck, C. (1986). *Persephone's Quest: Entheogens and the Origins of Religion.* New Haven, CT: Yale University Press.

White, R.W. (1959). Motivation reconsidered: The concept of competence. *Psychological Review, 66,* 297-333.

Williams, T. (2013). Saint Anselm. In E. N. Zalta (Ed.), *The Stanford Encyclopedia of Philosophy.*

Wimbush, V. I., & Valantasis, R. (1995). *Asceticism.* Oxford, England: Oxford University Press.

INDEX

U

unconscious mind, 8, 11, 14, 50, 58, 72, 73, 74, 75, 82, 84

universal goal, 11, 16, 156

upbringing, 20

V

values, 84, 85, 89, 139-140

vinaya, 59

virtues, 106, 107

vishru, 121

W

war, 54, 110, 135

warrior personality, 85, 135, 136, 140

Wasson, R. G., 79

wealth (incl. money), 18, 60, 127, 129

wonder, 41

wrath of god *(also see 16 basic desires/vengeance)*, 26, 55, 135, 143

Y

yoga, 80

Z

Zoroaster, 39

DEFINITIONS OF CONSTRUCTS
USED IN REISS'S THEORY

ASCETICISM
Austere lifestyle devoted to worshipping the divine.

AVERAGE BASIC DESIRE
Compared to population norms, an average prioritization of a basic desire. The desire may be experienced as high in some situations but low in other situations, or as neither high nor low in some or all situations. In the theory of 16 basic strivings for God, average basic desires have minimal significance for personality traits and spiritual experiences. They are virtually ignored in explaining religion.

BASIC DESIRE
A goal that motivates everyone and is deeply rooted in human nature. Also called intrinsic motive or psychological need. Basic desires have two parts: the goal (what is wanted), and the value (how much is typically wanted). In the theory of 16 basic desires everyone is naturally motivated to assert their values.

DESIRE PROFILE
The results of the RMP showing which basic desires are high, average, or low for the person completing the assessment.

FREE WILL
Opportunity to satisfy needs through secular or religious institutions.

HIGH (STRONG) BASIC DESIRE
Compared to population norms, an above-average prioritization of a basic desire. Typically implies that the desire is intense and that the individual seeks a high quantity or frequency of goal attainment. Example: A strong basic desire for power (1) may be experienced as a burning ambition, (2) implies high valuation of achievement, and (3) motivates people to seek a high degree of achievement.

LOW (WEAK) BASIC DESIRE
Compared to population norms, a below-average prioritization of a basic desire. Typically implies that the desire lacks intensity and that the individual seeks only a small or minimal quantity of goal attainment. Example: A weak basic desire for power (1) may be experienced as a lack of ambition, (2) implies low valuation of achievement, and (3) motivates people to be passive onlookers and non-interventionists.

MOTIVATION
The assertion of high and low values regarding universal goals. Low desires are just as important as high desires in motivating behavior. Only average desires are unimportant.

MYSTICAL EXPERIENCE
Altered state of consciousness of a greater or sacred reality.

PERSONALITY TRAIT
A deeply ingrained habit for repeatedly satisfying a basic desire.

REISS MOTIVATION PROFILE® (RMP)
1. A standardized psychological assessment of what motivates a person; 2. How an individual prioritizes 16 basic desires.

UNIVERSAL GOAL
A goal that motivates everybody (but not necessarily in the same way). Also called a universal reinforcement.